The Fish

WALK IN THE SPIRIT

By the same author

Power For The Body of Christ

As at the Beginning: The Twentieth Century Pentecostal Revival

Spiritual Warfare

Walk in the Spirit

by

MICHAEL HARPER

LOGOS INTERNATIONAL
PLAINFIELD, NEW JERSEY

Copyright © 1968 by Michael Harper
First printed in the United States 1970
ISBN 0-912106-70-0

Library of Congress
Catalog Card Number 78-135047

Reproduced from the Great Britain
Edition by arrangement with
Hodder and Stoughton, London E.C.4

Printed in the United States of America
Logos International, 185 North Avenue
Plainfield, New Jersey

CONTENTS

Introduction

CHAPTER ONE

INTRODUCTION

Since 1962 we have been meeting hundreds of Christians of all Churches who testify to a revolution in their lives. Nearly every day letters come from all over the world from people who either have had similar experiences, or who want to know more about it. It is difficult to know what to call it, but it is mushrooming up in the middle of our present Church situations. To some it is exciting, but to others it is bewildering in its comparative novelty. One common feature is the reappearance of the miraculous powers which marked the early days of the Christian Church. But there is an almost complete absence of the hysteria usually associated with these things. It is coming into the experiences of people of different classes, races and denominations. But it is much more than a renewal of the miraculous, there is a profounder love and joy radiating from these people. Christians are becoming more like the kind of people Paul wrote his letters to – yes, their faults as well as their virtues.

The purpose of writing this book is to try to help those who have come into touch with this new dimension. It may seem strange to those who so far do not understand the background. A car salesman does not give the handbook to a potential customer – with its detailed instructions about the electrical circuits and the kind of lubricant to use. Instead he will give him a glossy leaflet which informs him of the main advantages of the car. This book is mainly like the car handbook. It explains how to keep it running smoothly, and how to repair it if it breaks down. The next chapter has deliberately been included for those who would like to know what the great experience of the Holy Spirit is, and how one can receive it. Other books have been written if you should want to study the background to this whole subject, with accounts of people's experiences, and how these blessings have come to churches, and these, together with other books, are listed under "Further Reading" on page 96.

Dr Fison, the Bishop of Salisbury, has written: "The story of Acts is the story of the stupendous missionary achievement of a community inspired to make a continual series of creative experiments by the Pentecostal Spirit. Against a static church, unwilling to obey the guidance of the Spirit, no 'gates' of any sort are needed to oppose its movement, *for it does not move*. But against a church that is on the move, inspired by the Pentecostal Spirit, neither 'the gates of hell' nor any other gates can prevail."[1]

The early Christians knew what was meant by the term "the fullness of the Holy Spirit". When they came to appoint men to "serve tables", they picked "seven men of good repute, full of the Holy Spirit and wisdom". The apostles Peter and John detected something that was deficient in the experience of the new converts in Samaria, and so prayed that "they might receive the Holy Spirit". We may perhaps conjecture that a similarly obvious deficiency caused Paul to ask the disciples of John the Baptist in Ephesus the leading question, "Did you receive the Holy Spirit when you believed?" Lesslie Newbigin has put it very well: "Theologians today are afraid of the word 'experience'. I do not think it is possible to survey this NT evidence . . . without recognising that the NT writers are free from this fear. They regard the gift of the Holy Spirit as an event which can be unmistakably recognised."[2]

It is equally clear from the NT that the early Christian fellowships were richly endowed with spiritual gifts. Even when writing to the carnal church at Corinth Paul acknowledged that they were "not lacking in any spiritual gift" (1 Cor 1:7). He expected every member of the church to manifest at least one of these gifts "for the common good", and indeed urged them to bring their spiritual gifts to church with them. They seemed more concerned in those days with this kind of gift than with taking up collections.

The Acts of the Apostles makes embarrassing reading today, if we are right in believing that our churches should bear some resemblance to those early ones. The Church expanded in those days with a rapidity which shames most modern evangelism, in spite of all its up-to-date techniques and novel media for mass communication. Only in South America is anything comparable taking place, and it is not without significance that it is being done largely through Pentecostals, who recognise the importance of the Holy Spirit, and accept the gifts of the Spirit in their community life. The early Christians healed the sick and cast out evil spirits as an integral part of the Gospel of the Kingdom. In this they were following the example of their Master. It was more than a "battle for the mind", but a conflict involving the whole personality.

Thank God, we are seeing in our day the renewal of spiritual power in the lives of many Christians. It is springing from the recognition by many that we do not know the Holy Spirit as we should, and that it is possible, indeed imperative, to be filled with the Holy Spirit, and led by Him as the early Christians were. We do need a breath of fresh air, and as God sends it, so it will blow away many ecclesiastical cobwebs. This book is written to show how, having this experience, and, avoiding the dangerous shoals, we can steer a straight course as the Spirit Himself directs.

Receiving Power

CHAPTER TWO

RECEIVING POWER

Reading the New Testament we become immediately aware of a dynamic sadly lacking in much modern Christianity. Although there were no doubt exceptions even in the earliest stages of the Church's growth, the average church member possessed an enthusiasm which was contagious. The grace of God in baptism was not offered at cut prices, nor did they tailor their lives to fit the social and political structures of the day. They stood on their own feet, detached from the prevailing spirit of the world, yet wholly committed to its conversion and deeply involved in its life. That this dynamic was attributable to the Holy Spirit need hardly be stated, it is so obvious. There is no other explanation for the transformation of their lives in an otherwise impossible situation when Jesus Christ left them bereft and leaderless.

It is, therefore, of crucial importance to discover how these early Christians received the power of the Holy Spirit. For it is clear that what came so decisively at Pentecost was to be part of the essential character of the many Christian communities which were to spring up across Asia and Europe in the first half-century of the Christian era. How then did Jew or Gentile join the Church, and at what point did they receive the power of the Holy Spirit?

We must naturally start with the scene in Jerusalem on the Day of Pentecost. The great crowd on that day was face to face for the first time in history with a Spirit-filled church. It was reported that their reaction was one of amazement and perplexity. Alas, similar reactions are not generally provoked by the Church today. People may possibly be perplexed — but seldom amazed, for the wonder and sparkle are so often missing. Here, then, was the first-ever enquiry meeting — organised by God not man. They asked two main questions: "What does this mean?" and "What shall we do?"

It was Peter who answered their enquiries. As far as the first one was concerned, his answer was that this was the beginning of a new age to be lived in the power of the Spirit. What they, as Jews, had known in part under the Old Covenant they could all experience in full under the New. And as for what had just happened, this strange business of uneducated country bumpkins speaking fluently languages they had never learnt, this was accredited to the Lord Jesus Christ. For the One whom they had crucified God had exalted, and now He was pouring out what they were seeing and hearing.

The answer to the first question led to the asking of the second: "Brethren, what shall we do?" In passing, it is profoundly true that one of the reasons why few people ever get as far as asking us this second question is because there is so little to be seen in our lives to provoke them to ask the first, "What does *this* mean?"

So here were the first-ever enquirers "getting up

out of their seats". They had been convicted by the message they had heard. What could they do about it? Their second question was really two in one, and Peter answers both at the same time. The first part was, "What can we do to escape the guilt of having been responsible for the death of Christ?" The second part was, "How can we have the same experience of the Spirit, since you have told us that God's intention revealed in Joel's prophecy is that all should share it?" The answer to both parts was "Repent and be baptised every one of you in the name of Jesus Christ for the forgiveness of your sins; and you shall receive the gift of the Holy Spirit" (Acts 2:38).

Here Peter gives the only answer we may give to genuine enquirers. The whole of the NT substantiates these two facts: first, that the only entry into the benefits of the New Covenant is by repentance and baptism. And secondly, that the benefits of the New Covenant include the gift of the Holy Spirit as well as the forgiveness of sins. From Pentecost onwards the Church faithfully proclaimed that Christ forgives *and* baptises in the Holy Spirit. They taught that all who repent and believe are justified by faith, and that all who are justified by faith may receive the Holy Spirit by faith. The one should normally lead to the other.

It did for instance in Samaria (Acts 8:1–24) when, after those who heard Philip had believed and been baptised, Peter and John laid hands on them so that they might receive the Holy Spirit, "for it had not yet fallen on any of them, but they had only been baptised in the name of Jesus". Paul also had to wait for Ananias to minister to him before he was filled with the Spirit (Acts 9:17). And Paul himself led the disciples of John the Baptist, who were living in Ephesus, through full Christian initiation, first administering baptism and then laying hands on each of them so that they might receive the power of the Holy Spirit (Acts 19:1–7). Writing some years later to the same disciples, he reminded them of the incident and how they had been sealed with the Holy Spirit (Eph 1:13), and urged them not to grieve the Spirit, but rather to be continuously filled by Him (Eph 4:30, 5:18).

The only exception seems to have been Peter's mission to the Gentiles in the house of Cornelius (Acts 10). On this occasion they were baptised in the Spirit before they had been baptised in water. The normal work of the Spirit may have been telescoped too. This depends on whether they were regenerate (in the OT sense) before Peter had arrived. If not, then they seem to have been made a new creation in Christ by the Spirit, as well as baptised by Christ in the Spirit at the same moment.

It is perfectly clear why God worked in this unusual way on this occasion. Owing to the obtuseness of the Jewish Christians He chose to do something out of the ordinary to shake them out of their deep-seated prejudices towards the Gentiles. And it must always be allowed that God, in His absolute sovereignty, may choose to act in the same way today, bringing about the new birth and at the same time baptising new converts in the Holy Spirit. But normally this seems to take place, as it did in the NT, in two stages, however close in time they may be. The norm is set for us by the words of Peter at Pentecost. If Peter had said "repent *and believe* and you shall receive the gift of the Holy Spirit", then it could reasonably be argued that this gift is received the moment a person believes in Christ. But Peter said "repent and *be baptised*", which is different. Of course, Christian baptism presupposes faith in Christ, but the enquirers at Pentecost would have clearly understood what Peter meant by these words, namely that they would neither receive the forgiveness of sins nor the same experience as the 120, i.e. the baptism in the Spirit, until they had repented and been baptised in the name of Jesus Christ. Repentance and faith would have needed to be seen to be real before the early Church would have baptised anyone. But the point that is being made is that baptism takes time, whereas faith is instantaneous; therefore, Peter's words imply that some passage of time normally would elapse between baptism and receiving the baptism in the Spirit.

How to receive the power of the Spirit

Many Christians today are seeking God for the same promise that Christ made to the early disciples. They are not being disappointed. Either on their own in private prayer, or in company with others through the laying-on of hands, they are being filled with the Spirit, and often speaking in another language, as the disciples did on the day of Pentecost. This leads to a deepening of their devotional life,

greater love and joy in worship and witness, and effectiveness as members of the Body of Christ.

But how is this possible? Jesus Himself put it at its simplest and clearest when He said of the gift of the Holy Spirit, "If any one thirst, let him come to me and drink. He who believes in me, as the scripture has said, out of his heart shall flow rivers of living water" (John 7:37–8).

God's conditions

The basic condition Jesus makes is *thirst*. There is no doubt that it is this which is leading so many of God's people to seek for the fullness of the Spirit today. Thirst aptly describes their spiritual condition. Their life is like a desert. They feel dry and desiccated. They may have lost their first love, their enthusiasm for Jesus Christ and His service. They have more of the spirit of slavery than that of sonship. Their prayer life is dull and monotonous. So they long for the rivers of living water that can turn their desert into fruitfulness. It is clear from the words of Jesus that intellectual interest or conviction is not enough; important though this is it must be matched by that deep inner longing for reality and the power clearly promised to all Christians.

Another condition is repentance. John was later to write words which seem parallel to these other words of Jesus: "if any one does sin". A thirst for a holy God and to be filled with the *Holy* Spirit should make us aware of any sin we may be harbouring, and lead us to renounce it. But we must never forget that the power of the Holy Spirit is given to us *because* we are weak and sinful, to help us to triumph over this frailty and live joyfully and victoriously. Satan will try to hold us in the trap of self-examination. "It is an exhausting undertaking," writes Paul Tournier, "the mind becomes so engrossed in it that it loses its normal capacity for relationship with the world and with God. Locked in a narrow round of endless and sterile self-analysis, the person becomes shrunk and deformed, while false problems multiply *ad infinitum*."[3] St Francis de Sales has also written: "It is not possible that the Spirit of God should dwell in a mind that wishes to know much of what is happening within itself." We can torture ourselves with our vain attempts to interpret our motives and Satan will see to it that we never emerge from this vain pursuit. In our quest for this blessing the major requirement is what Jesus Himself called "a good and honest heart".

The source

It is most important to recognise that the source of power is not in an experience but in Jesus Christ Himself. It is not in the gift, but in the Giver. Jesus said, "If any one thirst, *let him come to me*". Jesus was announced by John the Baptist, when He first stepped on to the stage of His public ministry, as both the Lamb of God, who would take away the sin of the world, and the Baptiser (Greek *ho baptizon*: one who habitually baptises) in the Holy Spirit (John 1:29–33). We first come to Jesus with the sin problem, but we also come to Him with the problem of powerlessness. This baptism is His

B

prerogative, and He is the only Spirit-baptiser. On the day of Pentecost it was Jesus who poured out what the crowd saw and heard, and baptised them in the Holy Spirit; and it is Jesus who has officiated ever since in its administration. Men and women may be links in the chain that brings us into this great blessing, and it would be foolish to minimise the importance in this connection of the laying-on of hands declared in the Epistle to the Hebrews as one of the "elementary doctrines", but the Lord Jesus Christ is the One from whom we receive. If we already know Him as Lord, it should be easy for us to come to Him for this gift also.

Our response

Although Jesus is the source of this blessing, we have to make a response. We are to come to Him for it. This indicates a definite act of faith. Jesus issued this kind of invitation on other occasions too. "Come to me", He once said, "all who labour and are heavy-laden, and I will give you rest" (Mt 11:28). He also denounced those who refused to come to Him that they might have life (John 5:40). Faith is a key that unlocks many doors, not least to this blessing. Brinkmanship is a common attitude of mind in this connection, robbing us of what God longs to give us. We hover on the brink, instead of confidently receiving. We are assailed by doubts and fears. "Will it work?" "How can it happen to me?" "What will others think?" "Will I be able to keep it up?" "Am I worthy?" These are the kind of thoughts and questions which bombard our minds and neutralise our actions as we make our way to Christ. It all seems too good to be true, too simple to work.

But if God has promised, how can He break His word? So we come, humbly and honestly, to claim our birth-right. We shall not be disappointed. But if we doubt, as James has put it, "that person must not suppose that he will receive anything from the Lord" (James 1:8). A patient and persistent faith will bring us safely to the Lord who said "If any one thirst, let him come to me . . ."

Appropriation

If *thirst* is Jesus' condition for our coming to Him for power, then it follows that *drinking* will be the means of appropriation. Coming to a mountain stream and gazing at it will not slake our thirst. Admiring it will not do so either. Indeed the very sight of it will increase rather than diminish our craving for water. Coming to Jesus will not satisfy our spiritual thirst, if we fail then to drink or appropriate what is offered to us. Even worshipping Him will not avail, although this will assuredly follow after we have drunk. Jesus has told us to *drink*. This means to appropriate or receive what He offers to us – the power of the Holy Spirit. We do this by prayer – by the prayer of faith. To pray and go on praying is of little value, if we do not really believe we are going to receive, or if we are unprepared to come to a point of receiving, and then stop praying and start thanking and praising. The Chinese Christian Watchman Nee has written:

"Prayer turns to praise when the Holy Spirit has come."

We cannot dictate to God the exact moment of reception, and to pressurise Him, or to be pressurised by others, only indicates lack of faith, and may be dangerous. But if we believe in the promise, we know that a time will surely come when we shall receive, and know that we have received, the fullness of the Holy Spirit.

An outward and visible sign

It may have been the absence of the manifestation of speaking in tongues that prompted Peter and John to visit Samaria and pray for the newly baptised believers that they might also receive the Holy Spirit with the same gift as they had on the day of Pentecost. Dr Packer and the Rev Alan Stibbs suggest that the purpose of the visit of the Apostles was that the gift of tongues might be given.[4] But it is certain that it was this sign that convinced Peter and his friends that Cornelius and his neighbours and relatives had received their Pentecostal blessing. They knew that the gift of the Holy Spirit had been poured out upon the Gentiles, "*For* they heard them speaking in tongues and extolling God" (Acts 10:46).

There are some who insist that speaking in tongues is today the invariable initial evidence that a person has received or been filled with the Holy Spirit. But it is difficult to be dogmatic about this, for the only scriptural evidence we have at our disposal is a series of incidents in the Acts, and even this slender documentation is not conclusive. Larry Christenson also does not believe that a dogmatic case can be made from the New Testament evidence.[5]

All one can say is that it seems to have been the normal pattern in the NT that this gift was given when people were filled with the Holy Spirit. They seem to have expected it. This view is more fully expressed in *Power for the Body of Christ*.[6]

There is a real value in this gift initially to confirm to us that we have been baptised in the Spirit, and afterwards as a privately or sometimes publicly manifested gift for edification. Larry Christenson is very helpful here:[7]

To consummate one's experience of receiving the Holy Spirit by speaking in tongues gives it an objectivity. This has a definite value for one's continued walk in the Spirit, for speaking in tongues seems to have a definite bearing on the "pruning" and "refining" which a Christian must go through. I have wondered if the "tongue of fire" at Pentecost did not suggest that the "new tongue" they were about to receive would be a "refining fire" in their Christian experience. I find this suggestive in the light of John the Baptist's prophecy that Christ would baptise with the Holy Spirit *and with fire* . . . and the chaff he will burn with unquenchable fire (Mt 3:11, 12). This, at any rate, has been my own experience: speaking in tongues brings to my awareness many areas of my life which need pruning and refining — areas I was utterly oblivious to before.

Speaking in tongues is like a sacrament, an outward and visible sign of inward and spiritual grace. When someone has been filled with the Holy Spirit, the love of God is shed abroad in a new way in their heart. They begin to worship. Is it not natural, knowing the limitations of the human mind, that God should give at this juncture a gift or ability to express fluently what the heart is desperately wanting to say? The bottleneck is the human mind, which boggles at the wonder and majesty of God, and cannot keep up with the desires which surge up from our innermost being. The mind, wonderful mechanism that it is, can act like a dam when the rivers of living water flow from the heart. God is not a "dam-buster". The dam has an important function. Without the mind we would be like animals. But in those moments when "Jordan overflows its banks" the gift of tongues is a God-ordained channel or instrument temporarily by-passing or transcending the intellectual processes. Or, as Paul himself describes it, "If I pray in a tongue my spirit prays but my mind is unfruitful" (1 Cor 14:14). The NEB here translates the last words "lies fallow". Paul likens the mind to an arable field, which normally is used for sowing and reaping but is temporarily lying fallow.

It is of great significance that almost without exception the NT shows that the natural consequence of being filled with the Spirit is to speak. Jesus Himself expresses this principle when He said, "Out of the abundance of the heart the mouth speaks" (Mt 12:34). John the Baptist, who was filled with the Holy Spirit from birth, was described as a "voice crying in the wilderness", and the prophecy of Isaiah which Jesus fulfilled in the synagogue of Nazareth was concerned with One who, as a consequence of His anointing with the Spirit, would preach and proclaim a message. Elizabeth, Zechariah, Peter, Stephen, and Paul were all people who, when described as "full of the Holy Spirit", consequently began to speak. Then again, the prayer of the Church in Acts 4, which led to a fresh anointing with the Spirit, itself issued in a renewed boldness to preach the Word of God. It must be remembered also that the outpouring of the Spirit is prophesied by Joel in terms of language — "they shall prophesy". Then, the great exhortation of Paul in Ephesians to be continuously filled with the Spirit is linked directly with the use of the lips and mouth — "addressing one another in psalms and hymns and spiritual songs, singing and making melody to the Lord with all your heart" (Eph 5:18–19).

Although in the above examples it is to men that the utterances are usually made, it is surely not illogical that when men and women are initially filled and overflow in praise to God, that the gift of tongues should be given to enable this blessing to be appropriately expressed. This was, after all, the original intention of the gift when it was first bestowed at Pentecost.

But the important thing is not to concentrate on signs or consequences but on the thing signified. As you come thirsting to the source of all power, and drink, as Jesus commands, then rivers will begin to flow. This is the time to step out in faith, and in deep and humble gratitude to God for all His generosity and love, to begin to speak, trusting the Holy Spirit to give you the words to utter. Many Christians have taken this child-like step of faith, and found that "faithful is He who promises, who also will do it".

We should be under no delusions concerning what now lies ahead. Spiritual power is not given for our enjoyment. An Anglican vicar put it well when he described what happened when many of his church members were filled with the Holy Spirit: "We do not have less problems, but more; but we thank God they are now the problems of life, whereas before they were the problems of death."

These next chapters are concerned with some of these problems. A Christian who has no problems is probably back-sliding and almost certainly dangerously deluded. Jesus Himself went from His rich experience at Jordan, when He was anointed with the Holy Spirit and power, to face Satan in that lonely wilderness encounter. Yet He was not alone, for as well as the angels who ministered to Him, He had the power of the Spirit. Neither do we move out alone from our experience of the baptism in the Spirit. But we may be moving into a wilderness.

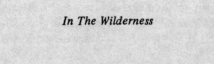

CHAPTER THREE

In The Wilderness

IN THE WILDERNESS

Many of the important stages in our lives as Christians are anticipated or followed by satanic attacks. It was strikingly true in the experience of Jesus Christ. When, for instance, that exciting moment came when the confession rang from the lips of Peter, "You are the Christ", He was soon having to say to the same disciple "Get behind me, Satan . . .". Or again, the agony of Golgotha was preceded by the agony in Gethsemane. But especially was this true of His temptations in the wilderness — for they were immediately preceded by His baptism by John in the river Jordan and His anointing with the Holy Spirit.

At the river Jordan God anointed Jesus with the power of the Holy Spirit for His future ministry. Together with this new power came fresh assurance — as He heard the voice of God saying "This is my beloved Son, with whom I am well pleased". This assured Him of His Father's love, His satisfaction with His life, and His divine Sonship. A similar experience often comes when we have been filled with the Spirit. We may hear no voice from heaven, but we do receive a deeper assurance of God's love for us, and of our status as His children. We experience this in a more intimate and personal way, and it strengthens our faith immeasurably for the work that lies ahead. The Puritans often wrote of this deeper kind of assurance, and linked it closely with what Paul refers to in Romans 8:16 — "the Spirit Himself bearing witness with our spirit that we are children of God". Thomas Goodwin, for example, wrote of it as "a light beyond the light of ordinary faith", and "it is faith elevated and raised up above its ordinary rate". "It is", he writes, "such a knowledge as whereby we know the whole is greater than the part, we do not stand discoursing. There is light that cometh and over-powereth a man's soul, and assureth him that God is his, and he is God's and that God loveth him from everlasting."

But this new assurance is often the precursor of deeper conflict and testing. For Jesus was "led up into the wilderness to be tempted by the devil" just after this experience. And one often meets Christians these days who have had a wilderness experience soon after the exhilaration of being filled with the Spirit. It may last for some time, but it is surely a privilege to travel along the same road as the Master.

Unbelief

The first temptation which Jesus faced in the desert wastes was directed at His faith. The words were still fresh in His mind — "This is my beloved Son" — when he heard the taunting words of Satan: "If you are the Son of God . . ." Again and again we shall be faced with a similar test. One often hears of people after they have been filled with the Holy Spirit doubting the reality of what has happened. Instead of believing the Word of God and His clear promises, they listen to Satan, or begin to assess their own feelings. It does not matter whether the experience received was dramatic or quiet, Satan is always at hand to challenge every good thing that God does for us, and every gift that He places in our hands. His methods have not changed since he more boldly contradicted God's word to Adam and Eve with the words, "You will not die". Throughout our lives we shall progress according to the degree we believe in and obey the Word of God rather than our natural reasoning or feelings.

As we have already seen, many people today receive the gift of speaking in tongues when they are filled with the Spirit or some time afterwards. Nearly always Satan challenges us when we first begin to exercise this gift. He will try to convince us that we made it up, or that we are "speaking in the flesh". It is surprising the number of victims there are to this temptation to unbelief. It may well be that whereas our first manifesting of this gift was accompanied by some excitement and emotion, when we come to exercise it the next day, it appears flat and cold. This is Satan's opportunity. The "if" of unbelief has deprived some, at all events temporarily, of the use of this gift. But this should be our cue to resist Satan. If we do fall into sin — and we need to remember that unbelief *is* sin (read carefully Heb 3:12 and Rom 14:23) — then the key to dealing with it is through confession and faith in the promise of forgiveness (e.g. 1 John 1:9).

Self-gratification

The link of that insidious little phrase "If you are" with turning stones into bread carries with it the suggestion that our Lord needed to prove his divine Sonship to Satan. The same temptation may well come to us. But surely we do not need to strive for signs to prove to others that we have been filled with the Spirit. It ought to be self-evident. If others do not see it clearly, then we might begin to wonder whether we have received the full blessing promised to us. But if we have, all we need to do is to believe, and the signs will follow without our having to conjure them up artificially.

We should notice that Christ's temptations began *after* the forty days had ended, so His physical hunger would have added to the temptation to use His new power for self-gratification. The parallel with ourselves may not at first sight be obvious. This is a temptation to use supernatural power for oneself, and so it is only strictly relevant to a person who believes that such power is possible. These temptations of Jesus are pre-eminently those of a Spirit-inspired person. It is only a person who believes in God's power to perform miracles who will be tempted to use them for his own ends. We shall, therefore, be wide open to this kind of temptation when we come to believe in and experience such miracles. For example, there may be a latent desire for self-gratification when we manifest one of the gifts of the Spirit. We may think it will give us greater "kudos" in the Christian fellowship.

It may even make us richer. Simon Magus saw what he could gain by possessing the power of the apostles. One has only to see the way in which the healing ministry can be used for financial exploitation to realise the dangers. We can launch into authoritative prayer for healing in order to build up our own reputations, and even powerful preaching can be regarded as a method for swelling our own congregations and making a name for ourselves. These subtle sins, mixed as they can be with pure motives, should be confessed and cleansed if we are not to grieve the Holy Spirit.

Self-display

The Lord was next taken to the pinnacle of the temple. Now this was in some respects a similar temptation to the previous one. It was prefaced by the same taunting words "If you are". Here, however, the temptation was one of proving to the public (not to Himself or to Satan, as in the previous temptation) by an act of supernatural preservation that He was the Son of God. He was tempted to perform a stunt, or induce a miracle. But Jesus refused. In the same way we may be tempted to dramatise or exaggerate our blessings. But it is a constant feature of God's workings that He never draws attention to Himself by unnatural means. His power is so great and so real that He does not need to. So also, if we have been filled with the Spirit and endued with power, there will be no need for us to do something spectacular to prove it to others or ourselves. For instance, there will be no need to shout or shake when preaching or prophesying. We do not need to assist the Holy Spirit in His work.

Perhaps a word of warning should be sounded here about testimonies. They are fashionable these days. They can be a real blessing. But they are also a potent source of temptation. Pride easily creeps in, stories can grow in the telling, and unworthy competition may lead to exaggerations and even complete fabrications. When Paul once had a deep experience of God, he referred to "things that cannot be told, which man may not utter" (2 Cor 12:4). Perhaps we too should keep some of our experiences to ourselves, and not allow the telling of them to be a snare to us or others. After all Jesus refused to allow His power to perform miracles to be advertised. His fame spread chiefly because those who had been blessed disobeyed His commands "to tell no man".

Although the first two temptations seem concerned with proving His divine Sonship, there is a revealing distinction. In the temptation to turn stones into bread His own personal desires were involved. But in this second temptation it is His ministry and calling which are at stake. It was a temptation to use carnal methods to achieve His ultimate purpose of saving the world. But the end never justifies the means, and Jesus rejected this suggestion. We too will know this kind of attack constantly. The more important the work to which we have been called, the more we shall be tempted at times to use un-worthy methods to ensure success. When we are short of money — and the work is threatened — how hard it is to resist the temptation to obtain money by unworthy means! It is all-important in our work for God to see that our methods are as pure as our objectives.

For Jesus this was also a temptation to act impulsively. The urge to throw oneself off a tall building is a well-known psychological phenomenon. We should beware of sudden impulses to do anything, especially those which appear unreasonable or even ridiculous. Guidance usually comes when we have had time to wait on God, and test the leadings which we may have had. The more important the action or decision the more surely He prepares us for its consequences. It is a mark, though, of Satan's tactics that he seeks to catch us unawares and trick us into thinking we have discerned God's voice when in reality we have done nothing of the kind. Recklessness is a mark of spiritual immaturity.

But this temptation was also one of "tempting providence" as we sometimes call it. It was a temptation to do something dangerous, to throw caution to the winds, to defy the divine laws of nature, and to do something unusual on the basis of a text taken out of its context. In quoting from Psalm 91:11-12 Satan significantly leaves out the words "to guard you in all your ways". The old axiom is true: "a text without the context is a pretext". Now, it is perfectly true that God does sometimes lead us to do the unusual. Jesus Himself may have been puzzled to find Himself shunted off into this desert siding when it would have been more natural to have pressed off along the main line of

His personal and public ministry. After all He had
waited thirty years to get started. But there will
always be a reason for the ways in which He leads
us, and we should beware of that glib and over-
simplified approach which so often marks the actions
of extremists.

When we have been filled with the Spirit we may
be tempted to travel down bizarre side-roads
occupied by fanatics. We may hear some very
strange doctrines and practices justified by deplor-
able exegesis of scripture. We may not be tempted
to throw ourselves off the tallest building in town,
but we may be tempted to forsake normal safety
precautions in the belief that now God will protect
us without such aids.

There are some who believe that they should sell
all they have and live by faith. Sadly such people
are often living on other people's faith. That some
are called to live this way there is no doubt. But
that it is exceptional and that such people should
receive overwhelming guidance and confirmation
concerning this is also clear from the NT, where
Paul deals sternly with those he calls "busybodies".
"If they will not work," he writes, "neither let them
eat" (2 Thess 3:10). It is salutary to see the example
of Paul himself, who "laboured with his hands"
rather than be a drain on church funds.

John Wesley was right when he said that pride is
the mother of fanaticism. It is human pride which
often lies behind the kind of exhibitionism which
this temptation represents. The desire to "put on
a good show" and to be conspicuous is a most un-

fortunate feature of much so-called "revivalism". It may be disguised with pious language, but the heart is still self-centred. Pride is also the root of much false teaching. The love for some unique doctrine or novel teaching which brings supposed fame to oneself. True balance springs from humility — and the ability to learn and take correction from others. And this will need to be more and more treasured as time goes on — for in the last days, we are warned, false prophets and teachers will abound, deceiving if possible even the elect.

Compromise

Satan took Jesus to another high place for his final assault. This time it was to a mountain. He showed Him the panoply of his great world empire, which was then very firmly in his hands. He promised to give all this to Christ, if He would but compromise once. Jesus knew that the purpose of His world mission was to regain possession of these very people and places. Now they were being offered to him "on a plate". But He knew that there was only one way in which they were to be reclaimed — through His own death at Calvary. There could be no compromise. He must go to Calvary. So Satan was again defeated, and left Jesus "for a season".

It must have been a shock to Jesus to find Himself faced with this kind of decision so soon after His anointing with the power of the Spirit. And it may come equally as a shock to us. In the first flush of the exultant joy of this experience, the call to suffering seems temporarily distant and out of focus.

C

Then we hear the words of Jesus: "Whoever would follow me, let him take up his cross daily". Power and suffering seem to be, at first sight, incompatible with each other. After we have been filled with the Spirit we begin to know in a new way what it means to be "more than conquerors". We may experience as Paul did that God "always leads us in triumph". We begin to tread Satan under our feet. It is just at this moment that we see the shadow of the cross on our pathway. What is it doing there?

To the apostles, power and suffering were indivisible. In the description which Paul gives us of his ministry, he refers to the Holy Spirit and the power of God, but also to "great endurance, afflictions, hardships, calamities, beatings" etc (2 Cor 6:3–10). In fact it was this suffering which, he says, distinguished true apostles from the false. It was suffering which was as much the secret of continuing power in the life of the Christian as the power of the Holy Spirit. In the days of the early Church, the new convert would not only start with this in view, but would have had to face the constant threat of death, punishment or imprisonment.

It may seem from the Gospel account that this temptation was too blatant to have held any real force with our Lord. But we have to bear in mind the intensity of His longing to win the world and the hideous suffering involved in God's way of winning it, from which, because He was truly man, He naturally shrank. Also, Satan was as yet undefeated and undisputed ruler of the world, and so was able to offer a shared dominion to our Lord.

"Fall down and worship me" seem strong words, until we realise that we virtually do this every time we disobey God.

The wilderness temptations, of course, were not the only ones that our Lord had to face. They were a foretaste of continuous conflict with the power of Satan. It was a battle which He was to win every time. And although our Lord went from the solitude of the wilderness into the hectic life of an itinerant ministry, the secret of this continuous victory was to be found in the life of prayer, which He was so careful to maintain. We too can share Jesus' victorious life, but to do so we must be prepared to share something of His private life of prayer.

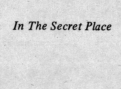

In The Secret Place

CHAPTER FOUR

IN THE SECRET PLACE

Jesus went from the loneliness of the forty days into three years of active public ministry. He packed into those years more than any of us will achieve in a life-time. Much of the time was spent in close touch with people. We too may find ourselves more busy than ever after we have been filled with the Holy Spirit. For one thing we shall have more to give. As our zeal increases we throw ourselves into God's work with greater enthusiasm than ever.

In this chapter and the next we are concerned first with the private and secret aspect of our lives, and then with the public and open. In this chapter we are concerned with some of the problems which face us in what someone has called "our solitariness" — what we are and what we do on our own. Not only shall we be dealing with our private devotional life, but with what is usually our greatest problem — ourselves. It is tragically possible to bounce along without really having come to terms with ourselves. After the first flush of blessing has subsided we will be disconcerted to discover that the old ego is still with us, and this will present problems to us — and to others. It can in fact mar all we do for God.

It is important to notice that our experience of the Holy Spirit can never be the same as Jesus'. This fact should save us from proud presumption. It is true there are many similarities, but there is one vital difference. The Holy Spirit at the Jordan came upon the spotless and sinless Son of God, with whom the Father was "well pleased". But at our baptism in the Spirit, the same Spirit comes upon a sinful human being with selfish concerns mingled with pure. It is significant that the Spirit came upon Jesus "as a dove". Gregory of Nyssa makes the interesting comment on the reason the dove was chosen — "because it has no gall, or else perhaps because the bird cannot endure any foul odour". On the other hand the promise of Jesus concerning the baptism in the Spirit is linked with the purifying symbol of "fire" — and on the day of Pentecost it was fire not the dove which was seen alighting on each of the disciples. In Matthew's Gospel, the words of John the Baptist make clear the purpose for which the fire is sent — "His winnowing fork is in His hand and He will clear His threshing floor and gather His wheat into the granary, but the chaff He will burn with unquenchable fire" (Mt 3:11–12). When we are filled with the Spirit there will be chaff left in us, which needs separating and consuming if the true fruit is to be pure. We must be open to the need for continued threshing, which may at times be painful. When our Lord came to the river Jordan for His baptism and anointing, He had long before "emptied Himself". He had surrendered His divine prerogatives. "Though He was rich, yet for our sakes He became poor." He sets us an example to follow, for we should have His mind — laying aside our rights as we surrender fully to Him.

Our ego

There is much need for real honesty — for if our ego is not dealt with, then our worship and service will be contaminated, perhaps in some serious ways. It is possible to be self-assertive while appearing to be led by the Spirit. It is only humility together with the necessary faith which safeguards us from speaking words as manifestations of the Spirit, for example, when the source is not the Spirit, but our own mind and emotions. Our natural reason and emotions can easily be mixed with the impulses of the Spirit, especially if there is knowledge of the matter concerned or some kind of emotional involvement. If, for instance, some loved one is very ill, it is easy to prophesy about their recovery without really being moved by the Spirit to do so. We do well to pray that God will divide the soul from the spirit and save us from this error (see Heb 4:12).

The baptism in the Spirit is not a short-cut to Christian maturity. Indeed it is often the signal for the breaking out of fresh conflict, which may well show us for the first time what we are really like. Just as the power manifested in the life of Jesus caused the evil spirit to cry out in the synagogue at Capernaum, so the new power we experience may provoke the flesh or our ego to new activity. "For the desires of the flesh are against the Spirit, and the desires of the Spirit are against the flesh; for these are opposed to each other, to prevent you from doing what you would", writes Paul in Gal 5:17. The resolving of this conflict is essential if the Holy Spirit is to have full control, carnality avoided, and the maximum glory given to our Lord Jesus Christ. One has been at meetings where the Holy Spirit has been grieved by testimonies which have been self-glorifying and by attempts to work the meeting up in excitement. There has been little sense of awe, yet it is claimed that this is "Pentecost". When the Spirit has full control, then we will not know where to put ourselves to get out of the limelight, so that we may all see the glory of God in Jesus Christ. It is tragically possible to receive a baptism in the Spirit and yet remain basically self-centred — a person out for kicks and the sensuous enjoyment of meetings, rather than the costly following of our Lord in self-denying zeal. It was to the gifted Corinthians that Paul had to write in 1 Cor 3:3, "you are still of the flesh".

Although it is possible to act like this, it will only be for a time. The power will soon be withdrawn and only human strength remain. The language will be there — maybe also the signs and wonders — but not the reality. Like Samson we may actually be unaware of God's strength departing. It is possible to go a certain distance with the blessing still upon us, but then the glory departs, for whatever we sow, we ultimately reap. "For he who sows to his own flesh will from the flesh reap corruption," Paul writes in Gal 6:8.

The NT has much to tell us about how this situation can be remedied. It abounds in encouragement as well as warnings. In fact the problem was met and decisively dealt with nearly two thousand years ago when Christ died on the Cross. This was more than the death of one — it constituted ours too. Paul recognised this fact: "I have been crucified with Christ," he testified to the Galatians (2:20) — "it is no longer I who live, but Christ who lives in me". Or to the Romans (6:6) he writes: "We know that our old self was crucified with him so that the sinful body might be destroyed, and we might no longer be enslaved to sin." We went down into the grave with Christ, so that sin might no longer have dominion over us. Paul does not exhort Christians to "die to self" — but he reminds them that they are already dead, and then urges them to live in the light of this fact. The exhortation to "put to death what is earthly in you" is based on the fact that "you have died, and your life is hid with Christ in God" (Col 3:3, 5). The well-known Chinese Christian, Watchman Nee, describes in one of his books what happened when this great truth dawned on him. He leaped out of his chair, and, running into the street, cried out with great joy to the startled bystanders "I'm dead! I'm dead!"[8] Sin is dealt with by Paul as if it is completely incongruous to the Christian. "How can we who died to sin still live in it?" he protests to the Roman Christians (6:2). A dead man does not fight for his rights, nor does he defend his reputation. As long as we are truly dead to ourselves, we shall not respond to the temptation to be resentful or revengeful.

Now, this is how it should be with us. But, alas, it sometimes is not. Are we, therefore, to conclude that Paul is day-dreaming, or that we are not to take these statements too literally? Certainly not! "It is not as though the Word of God had failed", as Paul explains to the Romans concerning another difficulty over interpretation (9:6). And we must beware of making the dangerous mistake of interpreting the Word by our own experience. On the other hand we must be realistic about sin and our own culpability. We must be honest and admit when we fail, and allow the Holy Spirit to search us and unravel the complicated skein of our motives and desires. The answer here lies in humble repentance, the real acknowledgement of what we are before God, and the confession of it, if need be, to others. Then there should be the definite embracing once more by faith of the clear statements of the Word. If we have thought, said or done something which is incongruous to the Christian, we should acknowledge it as sin, and then joyfully reclaim the promise, and our new status in Christ as those who died with Him.

Our life of prayer

The NT reveals that one of the most important functions of the Holy Spirit is to inspire our life of prayer. R. A. Torrey has put it this way: "It is the prayer that the Holy Spirit inspires that God the Father answers."

Paul often links the Holy Spirit with the activity of prayer. The best-known example perhaps is in Rom 8:26 when he tells us how the Spirit comes to our assistance in prayer. "Likewise the Spirit helps us in our weakness; for we do not know how to pray as we ought." No one by nature finds prayer easy, but the Spirit helps us. He gives us a desire to pray, shows us how to pray and reveals to us what to pray for.

No one can read the life of our Lord without being profoundly impressed by His life of prayer. Sometimes He would be all night in the mountains in prayer. If there has been kindled within us a desire to follow His example and faith "to do the works that He did", we cannot avoid the necessity of praying as He did. We must know more of His quiet hidden life of prayer.

If there is one clear rule for the maintaining of spiritual power and revival, then it is the necessity for effective and persevering prayer. There is no easy way round this. It is not prayer alone which brings blessings, but praying "in the Holy Spirit" which changes things. If there is not a greater depth to our prayer life after receiving the fullness of the Spirit, then we shall be missing part of the prime purpose of the enduement. It is so easy to miss this, for with increasing effectiveness there is a greater temptation to by-pass prayer. There are more people than ever in need of our ministry. We are more equipped to help them than we were before. But like Jesus we shall have to leave the needs of men at times, however desperate, to seek the face of God. For without constant contact with Him, power will be corrupted and the whole purpose of our work frustrated. Some Christians who have been filled with the Spirit have later had to make the sad confession that their prayer life has deteriorated rather than improved, and that they now spend less rather than more time in prayer. This should be put

right before God, if the purpose of this new power **is** to be fulfilled.

Praise

One of the most significant changes in the life of one who has been filled with the Holy Spirit is in the sphere of worship. A new dimension seems to be discovered in our relationship with God. We possess a new freedom and joy in expressing our worship. The gift of speaking in tongues is itself a means of expressing worship, a leaping past the limitations of the human mind, so that our tongue takes wings and the prosaic turns to poetry. One of the clearest marks of a true outpouring of the Spirit is the free and spontaneous worship which those affected offer to God, sometimes for hours on end. This should be expected and welcomed, for pure worship is the greatest function the children of God can ever perform. It has been said that "there is nothing like worship to disinfect us of egotism". Whether alone, or in company with others, whether "with the spirit" (i.e. using the gift of tongues) or "with the mind" (expressed in intelligible language), whether in silence or in words, whether with hymns or with prayers — this worship should constantly flow from our lives. It is an earnest of that fuller and purer worship with which we shall be occupied with the angels in heaven for all eternity.

Praise can also be a weapon for us to use against the enemy. The word "Judah" means "praise", and it is significant that in battle it was the tribe of Judah which marched at the head of the army. It was praise which brought victory to Jehoshaphat at a crucial moment (2 Chr 20:22). In these moments of worship we may lose sense of time and links with earth, as we are "lost in wonder, love and praise". This is no selfish pastime — it is the result of a deeper faith in God, and a source also of further faith. The spirit of worship so often springs from the assurance we have of His concern for us and His desire to answer our prayers. Worship in the early Church was also a potent weapon of evangelism. Before a word had been preached, the great crowd gathered on the day of Pentecost, when they overheard the Church praising God. "The joy of Jerusalem" was literally "heard afar off", when the 120 disciples were filled with the Spirit.

One of the main hindrances to worship is, ironically enough, prayer for ourselves or others. These concerns can become overweighted and out of proportion in our thinking. The reason for this is not hard to find, for the results of a time of prayer and supplication seem tangible. It appears that something definite is achieved by faith compared with time spent in worship. But this kind of assessment is not consistent with the mind of the Spirit. It is in the place of worship, when it is truly inspired by the Spirit, that we shall receive power from God, for we are released from selfish thoughts and unbelief. Such worship delivers our praying from being pedestrian — a kind of glorified shopping-list.

There is always a tension, as we have already seen, between the Spirit and the flesh. But Paul recognised another tension: between the Spirit and the law.

Our prayer life may from time to time oscillate between these two poles. One moment we may be in bondage to "law", in the form of prayer lists or programmes, and needing to enjoy the freedom of the Spirit. But then the freedom may begin to degenerate into laziness, and may need the discipline of form and order. Ideally, there should be room for harmony between the two, while always being open to fresh promptings of the Spirit, for He knows that we need variety and change in these things. Moreover, we may not know the dangers or burdens of others who are in need of prayer, but the Spirit knows how to intercede for the saints "according to the will of God". We should be ready then for unexpected guidance in prayer. How easily the mind sinks back after the stirring of the Holy Spirit to preconceived ideas, set ways, the planned routine and traditional attitudes. But the Holy Spirit will bring fresh and original light to the one who is continuously open to Him, with new and often unpredictable blessings.

Intercession

An interesting and sobering exercise is to compare time spent in prayer on ourselves, with prayer which is related to others. Satan always wants us to be unhealthily introspective. He wants us to be preoccupied with our own affairs, and especially our weaknesses, so that we have no time left for true spiritual warfare.

But intercession should be distinguished from supplication. The latter is concerned with "making our requests known before God". But intercession means mediating on behalf of or in the place of someone else. Where the need of a person is very great — when, for example, their life is affected by unnatural, grievous or evil circumstances, we may be called to go down into the valley, to suffer with them in the spirit, in order to bring about their deliverance through prayer. An example of this kind of prayer is given by Paul in Gal 4:19 when he reminds the Galatians, "I am again in travail until Christ be formed in you". Or in Rom 10:1, "my heart's desire and prayer to God for them is that they may be saved". In the previous chapter he has referred to his "great sorrow and unceasing anguish in my heart". Like another great intercessor, Moses, he is ready to offer the supreme sacrifice if only his prayer is answered; "for I could wish", he writes in Rom 9:3, "that I myself were accursed and cut off from Christ for the sake of my brethren, my kinsmen by race". He follows here the example of our Master in Gethsemane, who interceded for us as well as Himself with sweat "as drops of blood". This is a realm where few have fully entered, and none may enter without the Holy Spirit's leading and inspiration. With this kind of praying there is a real cost to pay, even physical, but we cannot expect Satan's strongholds to fall without it. When Jesus said to His disappointed and frustrated disciples, just after they had failed miserably, "this kind cannot be driven out by anything but prayer" (Mk 9:29), He was making it clear that some cases and situations demand more prayer than others. The same is true today. The prayer of faith will release one person in a matter of seconds, whereas in another situation it may be only after repeated and sustained prayer that the victory is won. We shall need discernment obviously to know what to do under different circumstances. In a similar fashion, some of the gifts of the Spirit may be manifested speedily and spontaneously, but other treasures will only come when we have fasted and prayed, sometimes for a period of time. For instance, we are told "at the end of ten days the word of the Lord came to Jeremiah" (Jer 42:7). Paul likened spiritual warfare to "wrestling" — and at times it will certainly be of the "all-in" variety.

Fasting

The NT does sometimes link prayer and fasting. For example, in Acts 13 we are told "after fasting and prayer they laid their hands on them (Paul and Barnabas) and sent them off". It was regularly practised by Paul (2 Cor 11:27 AV) and Jesus clearly regarded it as an integral part of the normal spiritual life, for in the Sermon on the Mount He links together the three religious duties, prayer, fasting and almsgiving, and assumes that the listeners practised them. Fasting linked with prayer in the Spirit is one of the secrets of spiritual power and effectiveness.

John Wesley in his Journals tell us of how the work of God was revived in one part of England when the Christians began to observe every Friday with fasting and prayer. He describes the result:

"God broke in upon them in a wonderful manner and His work has been increasing upon them ever since." He goes on to comment, "Is not the neglect of this plain duty (I mean fasting, ranked by our Lord with almsgiving and prayer) one general occasion of deadness among Christians? Can anyone willingly neglect it, and be guiltless?"

In view of this, it is alarming to discover that this important discipline has fallen into almost complete disuse in many Christian circles, being regarded as almost an optional extra for ascetics. It is good for the soul to abstain completely from food for a time, and incidentally it is often not without benefit from a purely medical point of view.

There may be times when we are faced with "mountains" which will only be moved by concentrated prayer and fasting. Therefore, apart from the regular disciplined practice of fasting, which we should adopt in our lives, the Holy Spirit may lead us into special times of prayer and fasting for guidance or more serious conflict with the power of Satan. We should not fast solely because of a sense of duty, any more than we should pray for that reason. But if we do sacrifice in this way, and in the right spirit, making it an offering to God, the extra time we shall be enabled to have in prayer will be wonderfully rewarding.

But now we should look more closely at the nature of the conflict we are involved in as Christians. And we must turn from the secret place of prayer and conflict with ourselves to the public ministry to which Christ calls and commissions us.

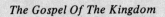

CHAPTER FIVE

The Gospel Of The Kingdom

THE GOSPEL OF THE KINGDOM

The hardest war to fight is the one without a front-line. Christian conflict is always like guerilla warfare. "The whole world," John writes, "is in the power of the evil one" (1 Jn 5:19). We are fighting in enemy-held territory. Satan snipes at us from every direction. There are enemy agents everywhere. The enemy has immense power and resources, and numerous allies.

We need to be made very much more aware of the subject of "the Kingdom", for it figured prominently in the teaching and work of Jesus. The word means "authority" or "the rule of God". When the noble-man, in Jesus' parable (Lk 19:11 ff), went into a far country to receive "a kingdom" (AV), it does not mean an area of land, but authority to rule. The RSV correctly translates the word "kingly power". According to Dr H. Ridderbos, the expression originated "with the late-Jewish expectation of the future in which it denoted the decisive intervention of God, ardently expected by Israel, to restore His people's fortunes and *liberate them from the power of their enemies*".[9]

God's world has been taken over by enemy troops. His concern is for its liberation. We are His troops fighting a non-stop and ruthless war, recapturing one stronghold after another from the enemy. This is what Jesus meant by the Kingdom. It is interesting that in the NT it seems at times to be almost synonymous with a word we are very much more familiar with: Gospel. For instance in Luke 9:2 Jesus commissioned the Twelve "to preach the Kingdom of God and to heal". They obeyed, yet in verse 6 we are told that they went through the villages "preaching *the Gospel* and healing everywhere". It seems as if the Gospel and the Kingdom are different aspects of the same thing — the reclaiming of the world for God, and the rescuing of men and women from the hands of the enemy. Jesus put these two words together in the expression "the Gospel of the Kingdom" (Mt 24:14). But if we do not link the Kingdom to our thinking about the Gospel, then we are losing something that is vital. For whereas the word "Gospel" signifies that it is "good news" that we proclaim, the adjunct "Kingdom" signifies what happens when we proclaim it — people are set free from the power of Satan.

The message that Jesus preached was centred on "the Kingdom". He was concerned with delivering people from the power of Satan. He was sent to "proclaim release to the captives and . . . to set at liberty those who are oppressed" (Lk 4:18). As He moved from town to town it was like the passage of an army of liberation. There was the woman "bound by Satan for eighteen years" whom Jesus released (Lk 13:10 ff.). There were the poor madmen out of whom He cast demons, so that He could say "the Kingdom of God has come upon you" (Mt 12:28). Disease and even death departed before the authoritative word of the Son of God.

The disciples also were given power and authority to do the same when they were sent out by Jesus. They too healed the sick and cast out evil spirits. They were told by Jesus that as they healed they were to declare, "The Kingdom of God has come near to you" (Lk 10:9). They came hastening back to the Lord with enthusiasm saying, "Even the demons are subject to us in your name!" (Lk 10:17). Paul and the other apostles had similar experiences after Pentecost. Paul himself was commissioned with the words, "I send you to open the eyes of the Gentiles, that they may turn from darkness to light and from the power of Satan to God" (Acts 26:17–18). He reminded the elders of Ephesus of his "preaching the Kingdom" in their midst (Acts 20:25). He was still preaching the same message the last time we hear of him in the Acts of the Apostles (28:31).

It is for this task that the power of the Holy Spirit is chiefly given.

Evangelism

It is fashionable to say that "the Church is Mission". We are soldiers in an army of liberation. If we are true Christians, we have ourselves experienced the joy of release and freedom which comes through faith in Jesus Christ. So, with a deep sense of our own gratitude, we join hands with others in the task of liberating the captives of Satan. Our enemy is a past master in the art of psychological warfare. He is the father of lies. He has infiltrated into the Church, and persuaded many to believe in his lies — even that he does not exist!

Paul describes Satan's work as "blinding the minds of the unbelievers to keep them from seeing the light of the Gospel of the glory of Christ" (2 Cor 4:4). The activity of Satan is massive and powerful in preventing people from believing the truth. He has succeeded in closing a third of the world's population to unrestricted missionary work. He has sent confusion into large areas of the Church so that few are clear as to what they should be preaching, and fewer still have any confidence in the Word of God. He has dangled enticing "red herrings" before the Church, so that some have become so pre-occupied with these that they have almost completely neglected the primary task of the Church: evangelism. Then even amongst those that are most active in evangelism, he has succeeded in blinding many to the full-orbed ministry of the Holy Spirit, without whom evangelism becomes a heart-breaking chore rather than an exciting adventure.

One of the most important purposes for the baptism in the Spirit is that we might have power to be witnesses to Christ. It makes possible our initiation into the strategy of the Spirit. Just as He was the inspiration behind the effective evangelism of the early Church, so He will be today.

We are not preaching to neutral forces, waiting to hear the Word of God before believing, but to people who are Satan's captives, although uncon-scious of it. It is the function of the Holy Spirit, working through channels that trust Him, to break these chains and deliver the prisoners. It is He, for instance, who convicts a person of sin, righteousness and judgement, words which modern man laughs at. It is the work of the Spirit to make Jesus Christ real to people — as the Son of God and Lord of all. Only then will they acknowledge His deity and surrender to His Lordship.

But the Spirit is not only concerned about the preparation of the listeners — He wants also to be the guide and director of the evangelists. It was He who moved Philip from a city to the desert, and called Paul and Barnabas to leave Antioch. It was He who told Peter to go to the Gentiles in Caesarea and directed Paul and Silas to Europe rather than Asia. As we wait on God the Holy Spirit will direct us in remarkable ways. Is there not too much man-centred evangelism today? May this not be the reason for the pitiable results so often? Is it not time for us to trust the Holy Spirit more?

Jesus told His disciples that the Holy Spirit would give them the words that they would need to speak in different circumstances (Mk 13:11). Expository preaching and courses on evangelism are important if the Word of God is to reach those for whom it is intended. But however faithful the exposition may be, and however good the training course is, they should never be substitutes for the Spirit. We need at all times the anointing power of the Spirit upon the words that we speak, if they are to be like "sharp two-edged swords" to our listeners.

But evangelism without compassion will never be really successful. Here again it is the Holy Spirit who helps us. He will give us that divine love which transforms evangelism into such a joyful work. He disturbs the complacency that is so often born of unbelief in the power of God into a fiery concern for the unconverted and unconvinced.

Healing

The Gospel of the Kingdom is also related to those who are sick in body and mind. Jesus did not divide people up as meticulously as some do today. His Gospel was for the whole man. He was concerned about their bodies as well as their souls. His salvation meant health to the whole personality. His Kingdom meant the overpowering of Satan in the realm of the body and mind as well as the spirit.

Even if we have had little or no interest in divine healing, the baptism in the Spirit brings us immediately into this sphere of conflict with Satan. Jesus was as indignant over sickness and disease, where it had been caused by Satan, as He was over sin and hypocrisy. He yearned to dismiss Satan from his position of authority in this realm as well as in every other. But He was careful not to form a healing cult around Himself. He forbade many of those He healed to tell others, and He related this healing power to every other part of human life. To one He forgave the sins before He healed the body, and to another He warned, "Sin no more that nothing worse befall you" (Jn 5:14).

The early Church continued to heal the sick and regarded it as part of the message of the Kingdom. And they did not regard it as a prerogative of an apostle. Stephen and Philip the evangelist, for instance, were much used in this ministry, and in the Epistle of James it is the elders of the church who are to be called by the sick man to pray and anoint him. It is important too to notice how often the Holy Spirit used the power of healing to arrest people and bring them to faith in Jesus Christ. When the early Church was forbidden to preach and teach, it is most significant that their prayer included both a request for boldness to preach the Gospel, and also that the hand of God might be stretched out "to heal, and signs and wonders are performed through the name of Thy holy servant Jesus" (Acts 4:30). Or again, it was the miracle of tongues at Pentecost, and the healing of the lame man at the gate of the temple shortly afterwards which drew the large crowds, thousands of whom were converted and added to the Church. Or again, in Samaria we are told that the people "gave heed to what was said by Philip, when they heard him *and saw the signs which he did*" (Acts 8:6). When Peter healed Aeneas at Lydda, the people who lived there "turned to the Lord" (Acts 9:35). The same results followed the raising of Tabitha — "it became known throughout all Joppa; and many believed in the Lord" (Acts 9:42). How can we neglect, as some do, this important ministry, when it has such enormous potential in communicating with the unbelieving world around us?

We surely need to have the same compassion towards the sick and indignation about illness as our Lord displayed during His earthly ministry. This is another area of spiritual warfare. Satan may sometimes trespass into God's territory here, too, and needs to be boldly and confidently evicted in the name of Jesus.

This is not to say that all illness is the work of Satan. We will need discernment to know how to act. Healing raises many problems, particularly concerning those who are not healed in spite of believing prayer. There is not space here to go into this in any detail. But it is easy to be glib about it all, either by dismissing this area from consideration and leaving it entirely in the hands of the medical profession, or by presuming too much. Nevertheless, it is important to discern the enemy in this field as well as others, so that he may be defeated and God's Kingdom ushered in.

Deliverance

Jesus specifically related the Kingdom to His ministry of exorcism, and we should do the same. He said, "if it is by the Spirit of God that I cast out demons, then the Kingdom of God has come upon you" (Mt 12:28). Part of Satan's power over this world and its people is through the agency of evil spirits. When Jesus sent out the Twelve and the Seventy He commissioned them to cast out demons as well as heal the sick, and this seems to have been part of the normal ministry of the early Church.

In recent years there has been a growing interest in this subject. Some of this has led to very real and successful exorcisms of people and places. However, it is a field of ministry into which we should only move with great caution. There are signs of a dangerous lack of balance by some who claim to have this ministry. This includes an exaggeration of the function of exorcism, and encouragement to some to take a morbid interest in the subject, bringing them into superstitious bondage, which can be spiritually harmful. This is no ministry for amateur demon-chasers, as the sons of Sceva discovered to their cost (Acts 19:13 ff). It calls for much prayer and self-discipline as the disciples found to their shame when they failed so signally in their attempt to deliver a young boy from demon power (Mt 17:14 ff). It calls for careful discernment, and much harm has been done already by irresponsible though sincere Christians, who have had very little experience in this field, claiming to discern evil spirits in people where there are none. This has been encouraged by some who teach that straightforward sins of the flesh, such as pride, anger and lust, are due to evil spirits. While this may be so in some cases, there is a need for the balance of the NT to be seen, where exorcism does not have the dominant place that some modern teachers would like to give it. There is much more emphasis on holiness and the life of self-discipline in the NT than on exorcism. A story is told about someone who met the devil in the street one day outside a church and he was weeping copiously. When asked what was the matter, he replied, "Why, it's these Christians, they blame me for everything".

Demon-possession takes place when the personality is "invaded" by an evil spirit, which remains there, at times overpowering that person. There may be more than one spirit involved. These attacks come in different ways. In some cases there may be physical manifestations — such as epilepsy. In others there may be abnormal or immoral behaviour, when the will of the person is completely bound. The evil spirit needs to be discerned, and if the person is willing to be delivered, the spirit should be cast out in the name of Jesus. Let it be repeated, this ministry can be dangerous, and is not for everyone. If in any doubt, it is best to find someone who has had experience in this field, rather than tackle the problem ourselves, which could do more harm than good. The after-care of a victim of evil spirits is essential, for there are counter-attacks to be dealt with, or the room which is "swept and garnished" can be repossessed by other spirits. The empty void must be filled with the Spirit, if the person is to survive further attacks, and the loving prayers of friends are all-important, as Satan is resisted, and the reclaimed ground defended.

But there is a similar ministry which is very much more common than demon-possession. This concerns dealing with what we might call "bondages". This is satanic power over some area of the life of a person. It may arise during early childhood, when an emotional crisis results in repression, with later psychological or even physical bondage. It may manifest itself in a variety of ways, such as irrational fears, shyness, indecisiveness, evil habits, depression, insomnia, etc. Satan has gained a foothold in the life, and it may well take the prayer of faith to dislodge him. It is wonderful to rest assured that any such spiritual bondage can be defeated and overthrown. Jesus said *"whatever* you bind on earth shall be bound in heaven, and whatever you loose on earth shall be loosed in heaven" (Mt 18:18). He gave His disciples authority to loose people from every kind of bondage in His name.

Part of this healing may involve the memories. Some need these to be cleansed and healed, otherwise Satan can use them to bring God's children into bondage, and cripple part of their spiritual life. Agnes Sanford has some very sound advice on this aspect of the subject.[10]

Social concern

There are many who view the theology of the Kingdom almost exclusively in terms of social concern. The roots of this can be traced to the Christian Socialism of F. D. Maurice, Charles Kingsley and others in the nineteenth century. It is fashionable to jibe at pietism as so "other wordly" that it fails to be deeply concerned with the real problems of life, such as racialism, war, hunger, etc. On the other hand modern exponents of the social gospel tend to be oblivious altogether of those aspects of the Kingdom outlined in this chapter.

True pietism, however, has in the past been deeply concerned with social matters, and their prophets have attacked social injustice and exalted social righteousness. The roots of modern British socialism stretch down to the seed-beds of Methodism, for instance.

Every one of us should be passionately concerned

about justice, public morality, and the plight of the under-nourished and under-privileged, and a balanced spirituality should reflect really deep commitment to the cause of man's physical as well as spiritual well-being. The Holy Spirit in the Acts of the Apostles was constantly destroying racial barriers, and reconciling deeply entrenched prejudices. It is important to notice too that in 1 Cor 12:13 the baptism in the Spirit is seen in this context. We often forget those words which follow the phrase "baptised into one Body" — "whether we be Jews or Gentiles, whether we be bond or free" (AV).

How we shall act in order to fulfil this concern is another matter and not within the scope of this book. But if we are to speak and act with authority in the sphere of social concern, then we not only need an accurate knowledge of the facts, but also prophetic insight and power which only God can supply.

. . .

If we are to be the children of the Kingdom in the fullest sense, then we should be those who know the liberating power of the Spirit ourselves, so that we can serve in the Kingdom of Christ. Then we are to proclaim to all the message of the Kingdom, and through prayer and the Word we shall see other lives delivered from the hands of Satan. We have seen the wide scope of this ministry. It is in this context that the gifts of the Spirit are so important. Without them we shall never be fully successful. We need particularly the gifts of discernment, the discerning of spirits, and the words of wisdom and knowledge, as well as the gifts of healing. But whether directly through their operation, or indirectly through the edification they bring to us, these gifts are weapons in spiritual warfare — and we need to be armed with them.

In the next chapter we shall be describing these gifts, which are reappearing so frequently in churches and fellowships. To many they may seem strange, but we should be thankful that God is once more bestowing them on His people.

For The Common Good

CHAPTER SIX

FOR THE COMMON GOOD

The generosity of God is patent throughout the Bible. He delights to give. He lavishes His gifts on His people. James tells us in his epistle that He is the giver of "every good endowment and every perfect gift". This divine benevolence, unlike much of its human counterpart, is entirely free from selfish motives.

There are many different kinds of gifts described in the NT, and all are important. But in this chapter we are concentrating on the gifts described by Paul in I Corinthians 12. This is not because they are more important than other gifts, but because they are so new to people today, and, therefore, need more explanation.

It is important for us as we look at the gifts described in 1 Cor 12 to realise that the nature of God, who *is* love, is inseparable from the demonstration of that love in gifts to us, who are the objects of that love. Dr Howard Ervin has put it this way, "Love is what God is. The gifts of the Spirit are what God does supernaturally, and it is a tragic heresy to dismember God. God never intended that He should be separated from His manifestations."

We should not, therefore, separate 1 Cor 12, which is about gifts, from 1 Cor 13, which is about love. Paul did not do this, for the chapters are an arbitrary division introduced later for the convenience of the readers. Both chapters are about God: chapter 12 is about His gifts, and chapter 13 about His love. But it was because the Corinthians were manifesting the gifts without love that he writes as he does. It would scarcely have crossed his mind that many generations later there would actually be Christians preaching love *without the gifts*. This modern deviation from the truth has a deceptive ring about it. It sounds very spiritual. "You cannot go wrong with love," some apologists argue, "but you can go wrong with gifts, which can easily lead to pride." But this attitude easily degenerates into false pietism. Dr Fison, Bishop of Salisbury, has put it this way: "The life Paul wrote about in 1 Cor 13 he expected to be lived in Corinth — and by first-generation converts at that! But he expected the life he wrote about in 1 Cor 12 to be lived there too. He was not prepared for a pietist clique of love."[11] "I just want Jesus" sounds very spiritual when taken in isolation, but it is contrary to the spirituality of the NT. Apparently, there were Christians in John's day who used very similar language, but the apostle deals very firmly with them: "If anyone says 'I love God' and hates his brother, he is a liar; for he who does not love his brother whom he has seen cannot love God whom he has not seen" (1 Jn 4:20). And John sees this brotherly love in very practical terms. If someone, for example, sees a brother in need and does nothing about it "how does God's love abide in him?" he asks (in 1 Jn 3:17). The "love" that dismisses spiritual gifts, as if they were superfluous, is not real love at all. In any case, these gifts are not for us, but for others, and, therefore, it is our brother who suffers if we do not manifest them. And we suffer also for Jesus said, "Give and it shall be given unto you". If we do not give, then we shall not receive.

Paul gives a number of lists of gifts for the Body of Christ, and it is wrong to confine them to the one list given us in 1 Cor 12. For instance, there are the ministries listed in Eph 4:11 and 1 Cor 12:28. There is another list in Rom 12:6–8, which happens to include one of the so-called spiritual gifts enumerated in 1 Cor 12. Nevertheless the list in 1 Cor 12 does have some special features which we need to look at carefully.

The gifts defined

Paul teaches in 1 Cor 12 that the gifts possess five characteristics. Each reveals a facet of their nature.

(1) *Pneumatika* — "spirituals". ("Now concerning spiritual gifts . . ." 1 Cor 12:1.) The word "gifts" is not in the manuscripts, and a literal translation is "now concerning the spirituals . . ." This means that they are spiritual endowments, and so to be distinguished from natural gifts. Such gifts should also be accepted in the life of the Church, provided they are sanctified and freed from motives of selfish ambition and pride. But the "spirituals" are gifts which exceed the natural, and may, therefore, be freely bestowed on members of a church irrespective of natural talents.

(2) *Charismata* — "gifts". ("Now there are varieties

of gifts . . ." 1 Cor 12:4, 9.) We get the adjective "charismatic" from this Greek noun. We can learn from this word that they are gifts and not rewards or wages. They are not prizes or badges given for special merit. They are freely bestowed upon the people of God according to the sovereign will of the Holy Spirit.

(3) *Diakoniai* — "services". ("There are varieties of service . . ." 1 Cor 12:5.) By this Paul implies that they are opportunities given to us to minister to others. They are another avenue of service, so that we can help others.

(4) *Energemata* — "powers". ("There are varieties of working . . ." 1 Cor 12:6.) This word indicates their essence: they are momentary powers rather than permanent endowments. They are bursts of spiritual "energy", which serve a useful purpose, and then disappear. For example, a person is healed through the gift of healing. The gift has fulfilled its function, God is glorified and it disappears.

(5) *Thanerosa* — "manifestations". ("To each is given the manifestation of the Spirit for the common good . . ." 1 Cor 12:7.) This indicates that they are not like the fruit of the Spirit, invisible graces, but rather visible acts which are seen, or heard, or felt. When Jesus turned water into wine, "He *manifested* His glory, and His disciples believed in Him" (John 2:11). This action enabled people to see His glory in action, and as a result some believed in Him. So it should be with every gift of the Spirit — a visible and tangible manifestation of the glory of God.

E

We can thus define the gifts of the Holy Spirit as: *certain powers (energemata) given to men by the Holy Spirit supernaturally (pneumatika) and freely (charismata), to be manifested (thanerosa) in ministry (diakoniai) to others for their edification.*

The gifts distinguished

It is not the purpose of this book to describe the gifts of the Spirit in any detail. This has been done quite adequately in larger books on the subject (see under "Further Reading"). But it does seem right to deal with some aspects of this subject which have not been covered by these other books.

Although the gifts of the Spirit bear the characteristics mentioned in the previous section, it is interesting to notice that the gift of tongues should in some respects be distinguished from the others. In the first place, it is the only new gift given to the Church by the Holy Spirit in the New Covenant. All the other eight were in operation during the days of the Old Covenant, including apparently the interpretation of tongues, for Daniel interpreted the writing on the wall (Dan 5:26). So far as we know there was no speaking in tongues by God's people prior to Pentecost, although there is evidence of it amongst devotees of pagan cults.

Secondly, the gift of tongues differs from the others in that it is a God-directed manifestation, man speaking to God, whereas the other gifts are ways in which God manifests His grace and love to men. Paul makes this point clear when he writes "one who speaks in a tongue speaks *not to men but to God*" (1 Cor 14:2). Even on the day of Pentecost itself the gift, contrary to the interpretation of some commentators, was of this character. The Church initially was speaking to God, for the crowd had not gathered when they first began to speak in tongues, they were simply eavesdropping on the Church at worship. It is true that they did understand the languages which were being spoken, but when Peter did address the crowd he spoke in Aramaic, a language which they all understood anyway.

Then, thirdly, the gift of tongues edifies the individual who exercises it, whereas the other gifts are said to edify the Church. It is only when the gift of tongues is coupled with that of interpretation that it edifies the Church, when it will be equivalent in value to prophecy. Paul makes this clear when he writes, "he who speaks in a tongue edifies himself, but he who prophesies edifies the Church" (1 Cor 14:4). One can now see why this is the one gift which Paul encourages the believer to desire for himself, and it is the one gift that can be exercised in one's private devotions. It is for this reason that Paul is anxious that all should possess it, even though only a fraction of those who have it will ever manifest it in public, when an interpretation will need to be given.

Some people would have us distinguish between 'higher" and "lower" gifts, and it does look at first sight as if Paul made such a distinction. He writes in 1 Cor 12:31 : "But earnestly desire the higher gifts. And I will show you a still more excellent way."

But this may be a wrong translation, for the Greek imperative can also be translated as an indicative: "but you do earnestly desire the higher gifts," etc. If we take this rendering Paul seems to be saying the exact opposite: he is criticising the Corinthians for desiring higher gifts rather than urging them to do so, as the imperative suggests. Now which is the correct translation? The usual rule for such exegetical dilemmas is to allow the context to decide the matter. Looking at this chapter as a whole it is the indicative which seems the better rendering. For if Paul is urging the Corinthians to desire "higher gifts" then he would appear to contradict much of what he has said earlier in this chapter.[12] His main argument in using the analogy of the human body is to emphasise that each member is equally important and dependent on the others, and that no one member should think of itself as "higher" or more important than the others. Indeed, God has given "the greater honour to the inferior part that there may be no discord in the body but that the members may have the same care for one another" (1 Cor 12:24-5). Gifts, like limbs of the human body, are functional in character. When we walk the legs are more important than the arms, and when we talk the mouth is more important than the ears. So it should be with spiritual gifts. Paul is not encouraging the Corinthians to grade the gifts, but rather he is rebuking them for doing so, and so neglecting "the more excellent way" of manifesting them. Clearly the gift of tongues was high on the list in the estimation of the Corinthians, and Paul wants to put it in its proper place, and

urges them to desire all the gifts, especially the ones **which** edify others.

However, it is still true that Paul does say that the person who prophesies is greater than the one who prays in tongues devotionally (1 Cor 14:5b); although if there is the dual manifestation of tongues and interpretation it is on the same level as prophecy. But this distinction that Paul makes is not so much in the intrinsic value of the gift itself, but rather in the fact that it edifies a number of people, whereas the privately used gift of tongues only edifies one person. Paul is applying here the divine principle, "it is more blessed to give than to receive". When others are present we should be more concerned about gifts which build them up than that which is a personal blessing only.

There is an apparent inconsistency in Paul's teaching about the gifts which has confused some people. On the one hand he seems to encourage speaking in tongues. He wants all the Corinthians to have this gift (1 Cor 14:5a). He thanks God that he has the gift himself, and used it prolifically (1 Cor 14:18). But on the other hand he puts severe restrictions on the gift in public, only permitting two or three to manifest it (1 Cor 14:27). The most satisfactory explanation for this is that Paul intended the gift to be exercised mainly in private. He undoubtedly used it often himself in this way, for he outdid even the Corinthians in his exercise of it.

It is most important that those who have received this gift should exercise it regularly in private. It is sad to meet Christians who have allowed it to drop into disuse. They lose, as a result, the edification which Paul says we receive when we pray in this way. It is a selfless form of strengthening, in which the mind is set completely free to worship and love God, without being hindered by the form of the words used. But we must go on to consider the operation of the gifts in fellowship with other Christians — when we come together.

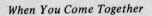

When You Come Together

CHAPTER SEVEN

WHEN YOU COME TOGETHER

One of the first problems which seems to face Christians after they have been filled with the Holy Spirit, and begun to speak in tongues, is how to go on into the experience of the other gifts.

It seems that there are three ingredients which need to be present if a church or fellowship is to reap the full benefit of the whole gamut of spiritual gifts. The first is *love*. Each member of the fellowship should be lovingly concerned for the welfare of the other members. "Love one another with brotherly affection", Paul exhorts the Christians in Rome — "outdo one another in showing honour" (12:10). "Do nothing from selfishness or conceit, but in humility count others better than yourselves. Let each of you look not only to his own interests, but also to the interests of others," he tells the Philippians (in 2:3 f). If these gifts are "for the common good", then a deep concern for others will be the best incentive for the gifts to be manifested. If we come to meetings only concerned for our own blessing, then we shall not be the right channels for the Holy Spirit to use to edify others. It is humility of mind, which Paul calls the mind of Christ in his letter to the Philippians, which is the essential basis of truly effective fellowship.

The second ingredient should be *faith*. As we have

already seen, these gifts are not human talents, but activities directly related to the Holy Spirit. Now the Holy Spirit never sets aside or overrides the human personality, as is the experience of spiritist mediums. When we manifest one of the vocal gifts, we do all the speaking, but the Spirit gives us the words to speak. On our side, faith is the essential quality required if these gifts are to be manifested. Paul tells the Romans (12:6), "if prophecy, *in proportion to our faith*". If there is little faith, there will be little or no prophecy. We shall deal later with the matter of how we know when we have an "anointing" to manifest a gift. But when we are prompted by the Spirit to do so, our active faith has to respond if the gift is to operate. As we speak, so more words will be given to us. A strong faith in God is essential if the gifts are to flourish in our churches. A timid and shy attitude will tend to quench the Spirit.

The third ingredient is *time*. We must allow time for the Holy Spirit to work in our midst. It is in this area that we often fail. The hastily conducted prayer meeting, the closely scheduled service of worship, the Christian with one eye on the clock all the time, will not experience the full blessings which God has for those of His children who take the trouble to wait long enough on Him. And, if such gatherings are closely packed with prayers, and there are no periods of silence, then the Holy Spirit will very probably not be able to speak through us. The still small voice will not be heard, and the message will not get through. Longer time together will never be wasted, for lack of concentrated prayer is a major source of weakness in our churches. One has also known occasions when a real spiritual breakthrough has been imminent, and the whole atmosphere has changed like a punctured balloon when a spiritually insensitive leader has interrupted, or an undiscerning Christian has prayed in an irrelevant or carnal fashion. The moments of greatest power in a meeting will very often be in those times of silence when we are most open to the Spirit's inspiration.

There are some definite hindrances too which need to be dealt with. Initially, for instance, it is easy to fall into this trap: because of the comparative novelty of such gifts and ministry, there may be a tendency to become so preoccupied with them that the whole purpose of meeting together is forgotten. The purpose should be to meet with God in worship and prayer, *not* to enjoy spiritual gifts for their own sake. In other words there can be a fatal concentration of attention on gifts instead of on the Giver. The results of this confusion may well be disastrous. Such meetings degenerate into little more than psychic fellowships. But no group need feel "cheated" if no spiritual gifts are manifested. These are the responsibility of the Holy Spirit and in His sovereign discretion He may choose to withhold such gifts temporarily, especially if *they* are becoming the centre of attraction. The Spirit desires to glorify the Son, and is jealous that He should have the pre-eminence in every meeting of God's people. The gifts should never become an end in themselves, or they will soon disappear.

Bad relationships will also be a hindrance to the operation of spiritual gifts. There must be a spirit of jealous regard for the corporate good. If we come to meetings or services with resentment in our hearts for others, or a spirit of criticism, or bad feeling against others, at best it will mar the blessing and power of the gathering, but at worst this unloving spirit can be mixed with the gifts, and the Spirit will be grieved. Damage may well be done to others. As Jesus, said "If you are offering your gift at the altar, and there remember that your brother has something against you, leave your gift there before the altar and go; first be reconciled to your brother, and then come and offer your gift" (Mt 5:23-4). If we have malice, spite or an uncharitable spirit, it will spoil what the Holy Spirit desires to do in such a gathering.

Decently and in order

Now a few practical points about the manner in which these gifts should be manifested. The principles have been clearly laid down by Paul: "Let all things be done for edification" and "all things should be done decently and in order" (1 Cor 14:26, 40). We have already covered the first of these, but the second is equally important.

Just as we hand presents graciously to those we love, wrapping them up at Christmas in bright coloured paper, and do not thrust them rudely at them, so we should manifest spiritual gifts "decently". This means we shall not shout unnaturally words of prophecy, nor speak so quietly that no one can properly hear us. It means we will not lay hands violently on people for healing, but gently and reverently. It needs to be said here that it is perhaps best for men to lay hands on men, and women on women, and the laying-on of hands should be carefully ordered in the churches. The minister and other leaders in each church should specify who should have this ministry. These checks are necessary because it is so obviously open to abuse. "Love is not arrogant or rude." We shall avoid the crudities of some, who shake people and in other ways manipulate them, and seem to show themselves impervious to the sensitivities of those to whom they are ministering.

We should also observe the principle of orderliness. "God is not a God of confusion but of peace," Paul reminds the Corinthians (1 Cor 14:33). We may receive, for example, an anointing to manifest a gift during a service, but that does not mean that we have to do so there and then. We can wait until an appropriate opportunity presents itself. In our walk in the Spirit we must try to be sensitive to the views and feelings of others, especially those whom Paul calls "unlearned" — which probably means those who do not understand or appreciate the gifts of the Spirit. The law of love should operate at all times.

Anointings

Some are perplexed as to when they should manifest one of the vocal gifts of the Spirit. How does one know, for instance, when the gift of tongues, which in its private use may be exercised as freely as prayer in English, should be manifested in public? Normally we do this when we have an "anointing" as many people call it. It may come to us in various ways, but generally speaking it is a kind of pressure to do it, which does not come from ourselves. It is never compulsive, a power forcing us to do something. For Paul says that "the spirits of the prophets are subject to the prophets" (1 Cor 14:32). This factor is one which distinguishes Christian gifts from the spiritist and occult, where there is a compelling spirit. There is often a feeling of discomfort until the gift is manifested. It is impossible to describe what is bound to be very subjective, but it will be made clear to us at the time, and we learn gradually from experience when this is. If it is prophecy or interpretation, then usually the first words are given to us; they come into our minds without pre-meditation, but with real persistence. We have to venture forth in faith, speaking out the words that are given before more words come to us. It is rather like the packets of cleaning tissues you buy in the shops, when one tissue is removed from the box, another one follows it, and so the process is repeated. We shall learn to be sensitive to the Holy Spirit and His lead to us to begin speaking. But we must not forget to accept His lead to *stop* speaking also at the right time. Some people, warming to their message, continue after the anointing has passed, and the message ceases to be edifying.

Things to avoid

One of the things to be avoided, which can constitute a hindrance, is the unnecessary perpetuating of traditional ways of operating the gifts of the Spirit. For example, sometimes people will preface or conclude a prophecy with the words "Thus saith the Lord". This is perfectly innocent and is intended as a kind of "signature tune" to prepare the listeners for what is to follow. But is it really necessary? It may be interpreted by some as being presumptuous to use the words of the Old Testament prophets. It may also lead people to accept a prophecy as possessing inerrancy. It is much harder to "weigh" what has been said, as Paul urges all listeners to do, when the person prophesying categorically states that it is the Lord speaking. It is perhaps better to leave these words out. But we should not deduce from this that God's voice has any less authority when He speaks through prophecy. A prophecy given at a meeting does not have universal and eternal application as scripture has. But the main difference is that when there is a prophecy I must judge whether it really is God speaking or not. But when I read the scriptures I know that it is God's word.

In some churches it is customary to punctuate prayers or sermons with loud "amens" and "halleluiahs", etc. This can be very distracting to the one who is leading in prayer or exhortation, as well as to the congregation, each member of which should be following what the one who is leading is saying. It has become a well-established tradition with some,

but it is another of those traditions which should not be imitated. It makes it very difficult for those unaccustomed to it to concentrate, and can quench the Spirit, since it all too often becomes an automatic reflex action and as ritualistic as mumbling prayers is to others. Words which are said without meaning them show an insensitiveness to the Holy Spirit. Another tradition to avoid is the practice of speaking in tongues during a meeting, without interpretation and in concert. This contradicts the command of Paul in 1 Cor 14:28. It may be edifying to the individual, but it certainly is not to the church, which is the reason why it is forbidden, since it breaks the scriptural principle for congregational worship: "Let *all* things be done for edification". Adherence to this rule is most important, otherwise meetings can develop into pandemonium, which grieves the Holy Spirit and offends many who are present, especially strangers. In moments of silence or at times when individual expressions of corporate worship are being used, it is still possible to pray in tongues without making a sound to distract others. Hannah is a good example here. We are told that as she continued "praying before the Lord", Eli the priest "observed her mouth. Hannah was speaking in her heart; only her lips moved, *and her voice was not heard*; therefore Eli took her to be a drunken woman" (1 Sam 1:13).

There does, however, seem to be one exception to this general rule. "Singing with the spirit", as Paul calls it in 1 Cor 14:15, is similar to speaking in tongues, only the Holy Spirit in this case inspires not only the words but the melody. As such it can be exercised in private (like a solo!) or in public, when many may be led to join in. The Holy Spirit becomes the choirmaster of a heavenly choir, and if the choirmaster is followed obediently, the resulting harmony of sound will be most edifying to those present, whether they are members of this choir or not.

Reverting to unhelpful traditions, John Wesley had to deal with similar problems, which, while fairly harmless in themselves, could be distracting to others. For instance, he refers in his Journals to the practice of "leaping up and down" which some of his more zealous members at times indulged in. "They are honest and upright men," he writes, "who really feel the love of God in their hearts. But they have little experience either of the ways of God or the devices of Satan. So he serves himself of their simplicity, in order to wear them out and to bring a discredit on the work of God." Maybe our approach should be as charitable and wise as that of John Wesley.

But we should all seek to be "naturally supernatural" as someone has put it. These gifts and manifestations should not be unusual, but part of the normal ministry of the Church. We should neither elevate them to a place of unscriptural prominence, nor grieve the Holy Spirit, who gives them to us, by denying their value or forbidding their operation. Let us neither fear nor despise them; and if God should choose to grant "extraordinary miracles" as He did at Ephesus, then let us praise Him for these too. But we shall not go far wrong if we obey the Pauline command to make love our aim and earnestly to desire the spiritual gifts, while at the same time applying his principles that everything should be done decently and in order and for the edification of the Church.

Members One Of Another

CHAPTER EIGHT

MEMBERS ONE OF ANOTHER

As Jesus moved around Palestine proclaiming in word and deed the Gospel of the Kingdom, He was obviously limited by His physical body. He could not be in two places at the same time. When He was healing the sick in Capernaum, He could not be preaching in Nazareth. His healing ministry was restricted, apart from the short missions of the Twelve and Seventy, to His own two hands and compassionate heart. And it is the same today. Jesus is still more or less restricted by His Body. The only difference now is that His Body can be in Capernaum and Nazareth at the same time, and indeed London and New York, or any other place you care to name. For the Church is the Body of Christ. It is important to notice that Paul does not say that the local church is *like* Jesus' Body, but that *it is* (1 Cor 12:27). We are His hands and feet, and humanly speaking, He continues His normal ministry through His Body — that is, the Church, either in its universal or local expressions.

There has been considerable theological debate about the meaning of the word "Body" in Paul's writings. But the fact remains that Christ and His people are inextricably bound together, and He continues His great work through His people whether we are His Body, in the sense I have de-

F   101

scribed it, or He is the Body. For an outline of the various arguments of the scholars see *The Body of Christ* by Alan Cole.[13]

This emphasises the need for both local church unity, and the functioning of the *whole* body. Jesus' body on earth was a perfect unity, with every part functioning properly, otherwise He would never have been able to do His work successfully. Only a local church functioning harmoniously is able to reveal to the world the full splendour of Christ. He cannot be seen fully in the life of a single individual. A group will always be a better witness than an individual.

Today, when so much is made of our "painful divisions", and when the emphasis is on the denominational aspect of this, we badly need to see also the harm that is caused by division in a local church or Christian fellowship. It may be harder to establish a true unity here than in the wider field of ecumenism. But it is in the local church situation that the more direct concentration of witness is being made, and it is this unity which is the special target of Satan's divisive tactics. When Paul was facing this kind of threat, he wrote "we are not ignorant of His designs".

Now this does have a practical bearing on our subject. For the almost automatic rejoinder by many when they hear of people receiving blessings and gifts of the Holy Spirit is, "It's divisive". Now, we must be honest. This certainly can be and has been divisive. On occasions it has severely hampered the work of God by splitting churches and fellowships into warring cliques. It is because of this that many regard the whole subject as distracting and unnecessary. We have to persuade people otherwise, for where there is love *on both sides* this is not divisive. For the essence of the Holy Spirit's work is to unite rather than divide the Body of Christ. The trouble in Corinth was caused by some who were making too much of the gift of tongues, and perhaps others who wanted to forbid this gift altogether. To the first Paul says: "Seek the other gifts, especially those that edify others", and to the others "Do not forbid speaking in tongues".

It is important to concentrate on the facts that unite Christians, rather than allow secondary considerations to divide. The basis of our unity is a common participation in Christ — the realisation that in Him we are "members one of another" *not* because we all have the same kind of spiritual experience. It may follow that those who have been filled with the Spirit experience a deeper level of fellowship. But the baptism in the Spirit should never be allowed to be the grounds for dividing Christians from one another. Any examination of revivals reveals the divisive tendencies which are endemic with such experiences. It is not long before the phrase "He is one of us" implies that cliquishness which we should do all we can to avoid. Max Warren writes of an important attitude of mind which we should cultivate towards the subject of revival, we should deliberately refuse: "to associate some inevitable connection between revival and schism. Experience suggests that we get what we genuinely expect. An attitude of humble expectancy towards the Holy Spirit in revival will bring a reformed and revived church."[14]

Above all we must carefully distinguish between the wheat and the chaff and not lump all together, which is, of course, a much easier way of dealing with the situation. Max Warren, in another section of his book, refuses to accept the inevitability of schism in revival. His words are worth weighing carefully, especially by those who are critical of any signs of "enthusiasm". He writes: "The Church has the difficult duty of accepting the challenge of reformation, while at the same time distinguishing between the challenge which must be accepted and the idiosyncrasies of 'enthusiasm' which should be tested and may be rejected".

The exercise of the gifts of the Spirit is sometimes raised as a reason for division. There are some who argue, "If you cannot exercise these gifts, you should leave your church or fellowship and join one where they are accepted". Some may even go further and say that if you do not do this you will be guilty of quenching the Spirit. Such an attitude is misguided, although it appears at first sight to be reasonable or even inevitable. Is it not based on false assumptions? The first is that spiritual gifts are essential to the Church. Now it is certainly true that they are essential for the proper functioning of the Body of Christ. Theologians sometimes distinguish between what is essential to the Church (the *esse*), and what is non-essential (the *bene esse*). Using this distinction we would say that the gifts of the Spirit are not essential to the existence of the Church, only to its well-being. The second false assumption is that *we* are quenching the Spirit if we do not manifest the gifts, even though it is in an unsympathetic fellowship. Under these circumstances surely it is *they* who are quenching the Spirit, not ourselves. For the gifts are for them, not for the ones who are manifesting them. If people are unprepared to accept these gifts, then we shall be guilty of quenching the Spirit of love if we force them on them before they are ready. Rather we should patiently pray that they will speedily come to see the value of them, and be prepared to accept them gratefully as gifts of God. In 1 Cor 13 Paul tells us that love "does not insist on its own way". To do so under these circumstances will hinder rather than help the work of the Spirit. Paul also defines love as being "patient and kind". If we shake the dust off our feet at our brethren, and move off somewhere else, what kind of love is that? The Holy Spirit is grieved by such impatience. At times we may well have to weep over the people of God, who refuse the blessings that God would give them, just as Jesus wept when He looked down on Jerusalem.

Nevertheless, the operation of the gifts of the Spirit within the normal fellowship of the Church should be our regular experience, and every church which is concerned to conform to the pattern of the NT should expect to see them manifested in an atmosphere of love, and be disappointed if they are not in evidence. The question is often asked as to whether or not these gifts should be manifested in the normal

church services on Sundays, or reserved for the
smaller mid-week gatherings. A quick look at the
NT should leave us in no doubt that they were as
much a part of regular worship as the Lord's Supper,
and no distinction is ever made between Sunday
and week-night meetings. Whenever the church
meets for fellowship the Holy Spirit may desire to
manifest some of the gifts. But our situation is very
different from those early days. For one thing, they
normally met in houses, not in large buildings where
it is so much harder to create the kind of atmosphere
where the gifts can operate freely. Vocal gifts will
not edify the congregation if they are inaudible to
most of those present. The ideal envisaged in 1 Cor 14
is full congregational worship, with every member
contributing to the edification of the whole body.
But owing to spiritual decline in the Church, and
the rise of ministerial domination, the proper
functioning of the local church, when it gathers
together, has been hopelessly stifled. The Church
of England is by no means the only culprit here.
Free Churches are equally hamstrung by the priestly
notion of the one-man ministry. But this situation
can be changed, and there are signs in a number of
directions that this is taking place. Those used to a
free type of service can easily allow more participation
by the congregation in the services of worship, and
the gifts of the Spirit can be manifested in such a
situation, while in the Church of England it has
already been demonstrated that there is no need to
dispense with the liturgy to make room for them.
In future services we ought to allow more scope for

an enlightened congregation to take part, as is indeed already being done in many churches. Extempore prayer should be allowed, and a time can easily be set apart for the exercise of spiritual gifts in either the communion service or the morning and evening services, provided, of course, the congregation understands what is going on, and is prepared to accept them as gifts of God.

In this connection, it is important to recognise the fact that the person who has the gift does not have to manifest it compulsively maybe at an inappropriate moment in the service. Paul makes it clear that the "spirits of prophets are subject to prophets". The person can wait until a suitable time is reached, and then manifest the gift. The gifts are for the whole local community, and are not primarily intended for a small and exclusive charismatic club outside the main fellowship. Anglicans are fortunate in possessing scriptural services, which form a splendid framework, within which the gifts of the Spirit can operate to the glory of God without detracting from the liturgy itself.

We should notice that Paul does not encourage an uncritical attitude to these manifestations. Gullibility is not a Christian virtue. The church is to judge the utterances of all its members by the touchstone of scripture, and this includes spiritual gifts as well as sermons. Paul says "test everything" (1 Thess 5:21). In an atmosphere of love, there should be no friction in such "judging". And the meeting together of God's people should be preserved from exploitation by those who like Diotrephes "love to have the pre-eminence" (3 John 9 AV). There are usually those who love to hear the sound of their own voices. A wise minister will lovingly restrain and counsel such people, and encourage the humbler and perhaps more diffident brethren to manifest their gifts for the building up of the Body.

It is an almost universal feature of the present wave of new blessing coming to God's people that there is an intense longing for deeper fellowship than is sometimes possible in our churches. It was true in East Africa in the revival — where the "saved" Christians, who became known as the *balokali*, met for special fellowship, where they could confess, testify and sing and praise their Lord. There is surely no harm in such meetings, as long as the dangers of divisiveness are remembered. If such a group develops in a local church, it should do so with the knowledge and permission of the minister and elders. There are few things more dangerous in a church than a secret society, which will be discovered sooner or later after rumours and misrepresentation have done their worst. Sometimes people may meet together who are members of different local churches. Again, there is nothing wrong, and indeed much blessing can flow from these meetings. But the dangers should not be forgotten. This kind of group can become a substitute for a local church, and would, therefore, sap rather than strengthen the churches. They can easily develop into "holy huddles", concerned only with a narrow aspect of truth, instead of fellowships where Christians can rekindle the gift of the Spirit within them, and go back to their local church with greater strength than they had before.

It must always be remembered that the power of the Holy Spirit is given primarily that we might be witnesses to Christ. Even the building up of the fellowship should have this intention rather than the cultivation of individual piety. And both evangelism and fellowship, as indeed all we do, should have the same great purpose, the glorification of the Son of God.

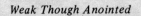

Weak Though Anointed

CHAPTER NINE

WEAK THOUGH ANOINTED

It was King David who, after the murder of Abner, said in his grief, "I am this day weak, though anointed King" (2 Sam 3:39). One of the great qualities of David was his constant recognition of his own weakness. Although God had conferred great power and authority upon him, he knew that in himself there was no strength.

The most dangerous condition we can ever get ourselves into is to imagine that we are strong. "Pride goes before destruction, and a haughty spirit before a fall," says the writer of the Proverbs (16:18). The baptism in the Spirit is not a mark of Christian superiority, but if anything it underlines our weakness. It is because we are weak that we have had to seek for God's anointing. And when we have been blessed we do not ourselves get an ounce stronger. It is only that God's strength is able to flow more freely through us. But the danger of human pride will lurk all the time in the shadow of our forward progress. Pride is a deadly sin, and great has been the fall of some who have become its victim after experiencing great spiritual blessing.

One of the clearest examples of this comes in the Old Testament. We are told about King Uzziah that "as long as he sought the Lord, God made him prosper" (2 Chr 26:5). We learn that "his

113

fame spread far, for he was marvellously helped, *till he was strong*". There was nothing wrong with that strength, for it had been given him by God. But there came a day when we read "he grew proud". He began to attribute his strength to himself, and it led to his ultimate destruction, exactly as the verse we have quoted from Proverbs shows.

But it is important to notice the form his pride took. He went into the temple to burn incense, which the sons of Aaron alone were permitted to do. They had been consecrated for that work. But Uzziah presumed that he could even approach God with impunity. He went beyond the bounds and forgot his human weakness and sin. His fall came when he thought he was too important and too spiritual. Even then, he might have escaped judgement. Azariah the priest and no less than eighty of his assistants followed the King into the temple and rebuked him. But the King was too proud to listen to advice and to admit inadequacy before such a company of "experts". He lost his temper, and immediately became a leper. His punishment was exclusion from the house of the Lord for the rest of his life.

This story has been re-enacted time and time again. It is being repeated in the lives of Christians today. God makes men and women strong in the power of the Holy Spirit. They prosper. And instead of constantly acknowledging their natural weakness and humbling themselves before God, they become first proud and then arrogant, and finally presumptuous in the presence of God. They become intoxicated with the wine of success and popularity. They think they are virtually inerrant and indestructible. Like Uzziah, they are angry when others, seeing pride in them, admonish them. They think themselves above correction. Then comes the sickening fall. They have gone too far, and they suffer the horrors of spiritual leprosy and so exclusion from God's blessing and service. As Paul warned the Corinthians, having preached to others they have become "disqualified" in the race of life (1 Cor 9:27).

Paul was an outstanding example of one who knew his own weaknesses, and counted only on God's strength. It was in the school of suffering that he learnt this supreme lesson, so that he thanked God for his thorn in the flesh, whatever that may have been. He did not come swaggering into Corinth on the crest of an advertising wave. "I was with you in weakness and in much fear and trembling," he reminded the Corinthians. But the results which flowed from his one-man mission put our evangelistic campaigns and missions to shame. Yet the converts he won in that city were later tempted to despise Paul because he had a weak physique, was unimpressive in appearance and his speech was "of no account". But Paul never gave up because of human weakness, nor did he become proud and presumptuous when God poured His power into his earthen vessel, as Paul himself called it, "to show that the transcendent power belongs to God and not to us" (2 Cor 4:7). He rejoiced in his weakness, for when he was weak, then he was strong (2 Cor 12:10). He would boast of his weaknesses rather than his strength, knowing that only then would the power of Christ rest upon him.

Hudson Taylor, the founder of one of the world's largest missionary societies and the first Protestant to evangelise inland China, knew this experience too, and never forgot it to his dying day. "All God's giants", he once wrote, "have been weak men who did great things for God because they reckoned on His being with them. They counted on God's faithfulness."

When we are baptised in the Spirit, we are just beginning. We are going to make many mistakes. We shall have our failures as well as successes and triumphs. But we must never allow these successes to make us proud. We must give God *all* the glory, and not talk too much about them. Nevertheless, we must never allow our failures to lead us to despair or resignation. They too should be stepping-stones along the way of faith rather than stumbling-blocks. If we are humble we shall learn from these mistakes. The proud man seldom acknowledges failure, and so never learns from it, for he thinks he knows all the answers. He will seldom take advice, and becomes angry when corrected. If we are going to be of any use to God, we must possess the humility to learn from others.

Though we have been anointed with the mighty Holy Spirit, we are still weak and "nothing good dwells within me, that is, in my flesh" (Rom 7:18). Every moment we need the presence and power of God. Jesus said (Jn 15:5), "apart from Me you can do nothing". The spirit is willing, but the flesh is weak, O so weak!

> Give me the love that leads the way,
> The faith that nothing can dismay,
> The hope no disappointments tire,
> The passion that will burn like fire.
> Let me not sink to be a clod:
> Make me Thy fuel, Flame of God.
> Amy Carmichael

REFERENCES

1 *Fire upon the Earth* (Edinburgh House Press 1958), p 79.

2 *Household of God* (SCM 1953).

3 *Meaning of Persons* (SCM 1957), p 68.

4 *The Spirit within you* (Hodder and Stoughton 1967), p 35.

5 *Speaking in Tongues, a gift for the Body of Christ* (Fountain Trust 1963), p 14.

6 *Power for the Body of Christ* (Fountain Trust 1964), pp 32–7.

7 *Ibid*, p 15.

8 *The Normal Christian Life* (Victory Press 1958).

9 *New Bible Dictionary* (IVF 1962), p 693.

10 *Healing Gifts of the Spirit* (Arthur James 1966), ch 7.

11 *Fire upon the Earth*, p 92.

12 Gerhard Iber takes this view of the verse, and has done research on the point. I am grateful to Arnold Bittlinger who first drew my attention to the matter. See *Gifts and Graces* (Hodder and Stoughton 1968), p 73.

13 Hodder and Stoughton 1964.

14 *Revival, an Enquiry* (SCM).

FURTHER READING

BACKGROUND

They speak with other tongues, John Sherrill (Hodder and Stoughton 1965)

As at the Beginning, Michael Harper (Hodder and Stoughton 1965)

The Cross and the Switchblade, John Sherrill and David Wilkerson (Hodder and Stoughton 1967)

THE HOLY SPIRIT

The Normal Christian Life, Watchman Nee (Victory Press 1958)

Sit, Walk, Stand, Watchman Nee (Victory Press 1957)

Power for the Body of Christ, Michael Harper (Fountain Trust 1964)

THE GIFTS OF THE HOLY SPIRIT

Concerning spiritual gifts, Donald Gee (Gospel Publishing House)

Gifts and graces, Arnold Bittlinger (Hodder and Stoughton 1968)

IN THE SAME SERIES — FURTHER READING

TA18 KATHRYN KUHLMAN — "AN HOUR WITH KATHRYN KUHLMAN"

TA19 KEVIN RANAGHAN, Author of "CATHOLIC PENTECOSTALS"

TA20 CHARLES SIMPSON — "A SOUTHERN BAPTIST LOOKS AT PENTECOST"

TA21 WILLARD CANTELON — "THE NEW WORLD MONEY SYSTEM"

TA22 THE CHARISMATIC RENEWAL —Bredesen, Ervin, Evans, Brown, Roberts

TA23 FR. JOSEPH ORSINI, Author of "HEAR MY CONFESSION"

TA24 PHIL SAINT, Author of "AMAZING SAINTS"

TA25 PAT ROBERTSON, Author of "SHOUT IF FROM THE HOUSETOPS"

TA26 MALCOLM SMITH, Author of "TURN YOUR BACK ON THE PROBLEM"

TA27 FRANK FOGLIO, Author of "HEY, GOD!"

RECORDS

MS120 AN HOUR WITH KATHRYN KUHLMAN $5.00

M7 NICKY CRUZ — 7" record $1.00

M13-72 NICKY CRUZ — 12" record $4.95

M125 NEW WORLD MONEY SYSTEM — Willard Cantelon $4.95

MS121 TAYLOR MADE CHARISMATIC MUSIC $4.95

order from your local bookstore
or W.B.S.
Box 292
Watchung, N.J. 07061

SUGGESTED INEXPENSIVE PAPERBACK BOOKS
WHEREVER PAPERBACKS ARE SOLD
OR USE ORDER FORM.

A NEW SONG—Boone	AA3	$ .95
AGLOW WITH THE SPIRIT—Frost	L326	.95
AMAZING SAINTS—Saint	L409	2.50
AND FORBID NOT TO SPEAK—Ervin	L329	.95
AND SIGNS FOLLOWED—Price	P002	1.50
ANGLES OF LIGHT?—Freeman	A506	.95
ANSWERS TO PRAISE—Carothers	L670	1.95
ARMSTRONG ERROR—DeLoach	L317	.95
AS AT THE BEGINNING—Harper	L721	.95
BAPTISM IN THE SPIRIT—Schep	L343	1.50
BAPTISM IN THE SPIRIT—BIBLICAL —Cockburn	16F	.65
BAPTISM OF FIRE—Harper	8F	.60
BAPTIZED IN ONE SPIRIT—Baker	1F	.60
BEN ISRAEL—Katz	A309	.95
BLACK TRACKS—Miles	A298	.95
BORN TO BURN—Wallace	A508	.95
CHALLENGING COUNTERFEIT—Gasson	L102	.95
COMING ALIVE—Buckingham	A501	.95
CONFESSIONS OF A HERETIC—Hunt	L31X	2.50
COUNSELOR TO COUNSELOR—Campbell	L335	1.50
CRISIS AMERICA—Otis	AA1	.95
DAYSPRING—White	L334	1.95
DISCOVERY (Booklet)—Frost	F71	.50
ERA OF THE SPIRIT—Williams	L322	1.95
15 STEPS OUT—Mumford	L106	1.50
FROM THE BELLY OF THE WHALE—White	A318	.95
GATHERED FOR POWER—Pulkingham	AA4	2.50
GOD BREAKS IN—Congdon	L313	1.95

POWER IN PRAISE—Carothers	L342	1.95
POWER FOR THE BODY—Harper	4F	.85
PREACHER WITH A BILLY CLUB—Asmuth	A209	.95
PRISON TO PRAISE—Carothers	A504	.95
PROPHECY A GIFT FOR THE BODY—Harper	2F	.65
PSEUDO CHRISTIANS—Jarman	A516	.95
REAL FAITH—Price	P000	1.50
RUN BABY RUN—Cruz	L101	.95
RUN BABY RUN—Cruz (Comic Book)		.20
SATAN SELLERS—Warnke	L794	2.50
SOUL PATROL—Bartlett	A500	.95
SPEAKING WITH GOD—Cantelon	L336	.95
SPIRIT BADE ME GO—DuPlessis	L325	.95
SPIRITUAL AND PHYSICAL HEALING —Price	P003	1.95
SPIRITUAL WARFARE—Harper	A505	.95
STRONGER THAN PRISON WALLS —Wurmbrand	A956	.95
TAKE ANOTHER LOOK—Mumford	L338	2.50
THERE'S MORE—Hall	L344	1.50
THESE ARE NOT DRUNKEN—Ervin	L105	2.50
THIS EARTH'S END—Benson	A513	.95
THIS WHICH YE SEE AND HEAR—Ervin	L728	1.95
TONGUES UNDER FIRE—Lillie	3F	.85
TURN YOUR BACK ON THE PROBLEM —Smith	L034	1.95
TWO WORLDS—Price	P004	1.95
UNDERGROUND SAINTS—Wurmbrand	U-1	.95
WALK IN THE SPIRIT—Harper	L319	.95
WE'VE BEEN ROBBED—Meloon	L339	1.50
YOU CAN KNOW GOD—Price	POO5	.75
YOUR NEW LOOK—Buckingham	A503	.95